AMERICA'S
TEST KITCHEN

THE
COMPLETE
COOKBOOK
FOR YOUNG CHEFS

sourcebooks
jabberwocky

Published by Sourcebooks Jabberwocky, an imprint of Sourcebooks, Inc.
P.O. Box 4410, Naperville, Illinois 60567-4410
(630) 961-3900
Fax: (630) 961-2168
sourcebooks.com

Source of Production: 1010 Printing International, North Point, Hong Kong, China
Date of Production: April 2020
Run Number: 5018771

Printed and bound in China.
OGP 10

CONTENTS

THE HAPPIEST MEALS ARE MADE AT HOME

Is there anything better than the smell of cookies baking in the oven? Cooking for yourself, your family, and your friends can be so much fun and so rewarding. You get to eat something delicious, and you get to feel good about making something with your hands and sharing your work.

Kid-tested and kid-approved means there are hundreds (thousands!) of other kids out there right now cooking these recipes, and loving the process and the results. When making this book, we had 750 kids just like you test all of the recipes to make sure you would love them too. Most cooked our recipes at home, sending in feedback on what tasted good (or didn't), what worked well, and what was tricky or just too difficult. In this book, you will also see dozens of kids who worked at America's Test Kitchen, cooking alongside our professional chefs. Thank you to all our young chef testers!

As you start to cook on your own, expect to need help or have questions (ask an adult) and expect to make mistakes (don't worry, we all do it!). Sometimes the worst mistakes end up being the best learning experiences. And remember, there's no such thing as being perfect—it just has to be perfect for YOU.

We made this book to share our expertise with a new generation of cooks. We hope it inspires you. Most of all, have fun and take pride in what you are about to accomplish.

HAPPY COOKING!

GETTING STARTED IN THE KITCHEN

UNDERSTANDING THE SYMBOLS IN THIS BOOK

To help you find the right recipe for you, this book relies on a system of symbols to designate skill level as well as type of cooking required.

1 hat
beginner recipe

2 hats
intermediate recipe

3 hats
advanced recipe

 = requires use of knife

 = requires use of microwave

 = requires use of stovetop

 = requires use of oven

 = no knives or heat required

HOW TO USE THE RECIPES IN THIS BOOK

Cooking from a recipe is actually a three-step process, and the recipes in this book are written to reflect that, with three distinct sections. Preparing your ingredients in advance and gathering equipment before you cook reduces mistakes because you won't be hunting around the kitchen for an ingredient or tool while food is cooking in a pan or heating in the oven.

PREPARE INGREDIENTS: Start with the list of ingredients and prepare them as directed. Measure ingredients and chop as needed. Wash fruits and vegetables. Use prep bowls to keep ingredients organized.

GATHER COOKING EQUIPMENT: Once all your ingredients are ready, put all the cooking tools you will need to follow the recipe instructions on the counter.

START COOKING!: It's finally time to mix ingredients together and heat things on the stovetop or in the oven. Put your phone away and save homework for later. You're cooking!

4 SECRETS TO SUCCESS IN THE KITCHEN

Cooking is not rocket science. Humans have been cooking since we learned to control fire more than one million years ago. That's a lot of mac and cheese! What cooking does require is attention to detail. Here are four secrets to becoming a kitchen pro.

SECRET #1: READ CAREFULLY

If you're learning to cook, chances are you are reading a recipe. It will take some time to understand the language used in recipes (see "Decoding Kitchenspeak," page 8).

• Start with the key stats. How much food does the recipe make? How long will it take? When you're hungry for an after-school snack, choose a recipe that serves one or two people (not four) and takes 15 minutes to prepare rather than an hour.

• Make sure you have the right ingredients and equipment. Don't start a guacamole recipe only to realize there are no avocados in your kitchen. Likewise, don't prepare the batter for a cake before making sure you have the right size cake pan.

• Follow the recipe as written, at least the first time. You can always improvise once you understand how the recipe works. See the "Make It Your Way" sidebars for suggestions on how to customize recipes to suit your taste.

SECRET #2: STAY FOCUSED

Cooking requires the active participation of the cook.

• Measure carefully (see page 11 for tips). Too much salt can ruin a recipe. Too little broth and the rice can burn.

• Recipes are written with both times ("cook for 5 minutes") and visual cues ("cook until golden brown"). Good cooks use all their senses—sight, hearing, touch, smell, and taste—in the kitchen.

• Many recipes contain time ranges, such as "cook until brown, 20 to 25 minutes." These ranges account for differences in various stovetops or ovens. Set your timer for the lower number. If the food isn't done when the timer goes off, you can always keep cooking and reset the timer. But once food is overcooked, there's no going back.

SECRET #3: PRACTICE SAFETY

Yes, knives and stoves can be dangerous. Always ask for help if you're in doubt.

• Use the knife that's right for you. This will depend on the size of your hands and your skill level (see page 121 for recommendations). Learn how to hold and use a knife (see page 122 for tips).

• Hot stovetops and ovens can cause painful burns. Assume that anything on the stovetop (including the pan's handle and lid) is hot. Everything inside the oven is definitely hot. Always use oven mitts (see page 87 for recommendations).

• Wash your hands before cooking.

• Wash your hands after touching raw meat, chicken, fish, or eggs.

• Never let foods you eat raw (such as salad) touch foods you will cook (such as chicken). For example, don't prepare raw meat and then use the same cutting board to slice veggies.

• Don't ever leave something on the stove unattended. Always turn off the stove and oven when you're done.

SECRET #4: MISTAKES ARE OK

Making mistakes is a great way to learn.

• Try to figure out what you would do differently next time. Maybe you should have set a timer so you would remember to check the cookies in the oven. Maybe you should have measured more carefully.

• If your food isn't perfect, don't worry. A misshapen cookie is still delicious. If you enjoy your "mistakes," everyone else will enjoy them, too. Remember: You cooked! That's so cool.

→ DECODING KITCHENSPEAK ←

Reading a recipe can sometimes feel like reading a foreign language. Here are some common words in many cookbooks and what they really mean.

THINGS YOU DO WITH A SHARP TOOL

PEEL: To remove the outer skin, rind, or layer from food, usually a piece of fruit or a vegetable. Often done with a vegetable peeler.

ZEST: To remove the flavorful colored outer peel from a lemon, lime, or orange (the colored skin is called the zest). Does not include the bitter white layer (called pith) under the zest.

CHOP: To cut food with a knife into small pieces. *Chopped fine* = ⅛- to ¼-inch pieces. *Chopped* = ¼- to ½-inch pieces. *Chopped coarse* = ½- to ¾-inch pieces. Use a ruler to understand the different sizes.

MINCE: To cut food with a knife into ⅛-inch pieces or smaller.

SLICE: To cut food with a knife into pieces with two flat sides, with the thickness dependent on the recipe instructions. For example, slicing a celery stalk.

GRATE: To cut food (often cheese) into very small, uniform pieces using a rasp grater or the small holes on a box grater.

SHRED: To cut food (often cheese but also some vegetables and fruits) into small, uniform pieces using the large holes on a box grater or the shredding disk of a food processor.

THINGS YOU DO IN A BOWL

STIR: To combine ingredients in a bowl or cooking vessel, often with a rubber spatula or wooden spoon.

TOSS: To gently combine ingredients with tongs or two forks and/or spoons in order to distribute the ingredients evenly. You toss salad in a bowl (you don't stir it).

WHISK: To combine ingredients with a whisk until uniform or evenly incorporated. For example, you whisk whole eggs before scrambling them.

BEAT: To combine vigorously with a whisk, fork, or electric mixer, often with the goal of adding air to increase the volume of the ingredients (such as beating butter and sugar together to make cookie dough).

WHIP: To combine vigorously with a whisk or electric mixer, with the goal of adding air to increase the volume of the ingredients (such as whipping cream or egg whites).

SCRAPE: To push ingredients on the sides of a bowl, pan, blender jar, or food processor back into the center. A rubber spatula is the best tool for this job.

THINGS YOU DO WITH HEAT

MELT: To heat solid food (think butter) on the stovetop or in the microwave until it becomes a liquid.

HEAT UNTIL SHIMMERING: To heat oil in a pan until it begins to move slightly, which indicates the oil is hot enough for cooking. If the oil starts to smoke, it has been overheated, and you should start over with fresh oil.

SIMMER: To heat liquid until small bubbles gently break the surface at a variable and infrequent rate, as when cooking a soup.

BOIL: To heat liquid until large bubbles break the surface at a rapid and constant rate, as when cooking pasta.

TOAST: To heat food (often nuts or bread) in a skillet, toaster, or oven until golden brown and fragrant.

TASTE BEFORE YOU SERVE

Many recipes say "season to taste" just before serving. What does this mean? "Seasoning" means salt and pepper. Different people have different tastes. Maybe your little brother doesn't like pepper. Seasoning just before serving lets you control how much salt and pepper go into your food. You can also adjust the flavors with other ingredients:

• Drizzle soups, pastas, vegetables, and fish with **extra-virgin olive oil** for a last-minute hit of flavor and richness.

• Sprinkle almost anything with **minced fresh herbs**. Parsley and chives are favorites, but cilantro works in many recipes, and basil is a classic in Italian cooking.

• Squeeze a little **lemon juice** over simple chicken or fish dishes, vegetables, or even a bowl of soup for a squirt of brightness.

• Stir in a dash of heat by adding a pinch of **red pepper flakes** to sauces, soups, and stews.

WHAT'S UP WITH INGREDIENTS?

A well-stocked pantry means you are ready to cook. Here are items to keep on hand, with notes on what to buy.

SALT: There are many kinds of salt. Recipes in this book were tested with table salt (the kind with fine crystals that you keep in a shaker). You can use larger, chunkier kosher salt or sea salt, but you may need a bit more of it.

PEPPER: Whole peppercorns freshly ground in a pepper mill are much more flavorful than the ground pepper you buy in the supermarket.

OIL: Use extra-virgin olive oil in recipes where the flavor of the oil is important, such as salad dressing. Bland vegetable oil is useful in many cooking and baking recipes.

 BUTTER: Use unsalted butter. Salted butter is great on toast but can make some foods too salty.

EGGS: Most recipes call for large eggs. You can use different sizes in egg dishes (such as an omelet), but in baking recipes use the size the recipe calls for.

MILK & DAIRY: Milk, cream, half-and-half (made with half milk and half cream), yogurt, and sour cream are common ingredients. While low-fat milk and whole milk will work the same way in most recipes, don't use milk in a recipe that calls for cream.

BROTH: Store-bought chicken broth and vegetable broth can be used interchangeably in most recipes.

HERBS: Fresh herbs add so much more flavor to dishes than dried ones. Dried oregano and thyme are OK, but don't bother with dried parsley, basil, or cilantro (they taste like sawdust). See page 53 to learn more about fresh herbs.

SPICES: Ground spices, such as cumin and chili powder, add flavor in a flash. Keep spices in the pantry for up to one year, and then buy fresh jars.

 GARLIC & ONIONS: Many recipes call for garlic and/or onions. These flavorful ingredients require special prep (see page 13) and should be stored in the pantry, not the fridge.

BAKING POWDER & BAKING SODA: These leaveners are essential in pancakes, muffins, cakes, cookies, and more. They are not interchangeable. See page 144 to learn how these powders help baked goods rise.

FLOUR: Stock all-purpose flour in your pantry—it works well in a wide range of recipes, from cakes to cookies.

SUGAR: Granulated white sugar is the most commonly used sweetener, although some recipes call for confectioners' sugar or brown sugar (use either light or dark unless the recipe specifies otherwise).

HOW TO MEASURE

For consistent results, it's important to measure accurately. Dry ingredients and liquid ingredients are measured differently. Note that small amounts of both dry and liquid ingredients are measured with small measuring spoons.

DRY INGREDIENTS (everything from flour and sugar to rice and frozen peas) should be measured in dry measuring cups—small metal or plastic cups with handles. Each set has cups of varying sizes—¼ cup, ⅓ cup, ½ cup, and 1 cup are standard. Dip the measuring cup into the ingredient and sweep away the excess with the back of a butter knife.

LIQUID INGREDIENTS (milk, water, juice) should be measured in a liquid measuring cup (a larger, clear plastic or glass cup with lines on the side, a big handle, and a pour spout). Set the measuring cup level on the counter and bend down to read the bottom of the concave arc at the liquid's surface. This is known as the meniscus line.

KITCHEN MATH

You can get carried away learning all the math behind measuring. Memorize the following rules, and you will be set.

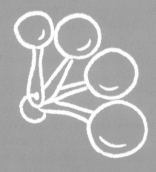

3 TEASPOONS = 1 TABLESPOON

16 TABLESPOONS = 1 CUP

16 OUNCES = 1 POUND

7 ESSENTIAL PREP STEPS

Most ingredients must be prepared before they can be used in a recipe. Learn how to prepare the seven ingredients highlighted on the following pages and you will be able to make so many recipes.

HOW TO CRACK AND SEPARATE EGGS

Unless you are hard-cooking eggs, you need to start by cracking them open. In some recipes, you will need to separate the yolk (the yellow part) and white (the clear part) and use them differently. Cold eggs are much easier to separate.

1. To crack: Gently hit side of egg against flat surface of counter or cutting board.

2. Pull shell apart into 2 pieces over bowl. Let yolk and white drop into bowl. Discard shell.

3. To separate yolk and white: Use your hand to very gently transfer yolk to second bowl.

HOW TO MELT BUTTER

Butter can be melted in a small saucepan on the stove (use medium-low heat), but we think the microwave is easier.

1. Cut butter into 1-tablespoon pieces. Place butter in microwave-safe bowl.

2. Place bowl in microwave and cover bowl with small plate. Use 50 percent power to heat butter until melted, 30 to 60 seconds (longer if melting a lot of butter). Watch butter and stop microwave as soon as butter has melted. Use oven mitts to remove bowl from microwave.

HOW TO MINCE GARLIC

Garlic is sticky, so you may need to carefully wipe it from the sides of the knife to get the pieces of garlic back onto the cutting board, where you can cut them. You can also use a garlic press to both peel and mince garlic—so easy.

1. Crush clove with bottom of measuring cup to loosen papery skin. Use your fingers to remove and discard papery skin.

2. Place one hand on handle of chef's knife and rest fingers of your other hand on top of blade. Use rocking motion, pivoting knife as you chop garlic repeatedly to cut it into very small pieces.

HOW TO CHOP FRESH HERBS

Fresh herbs need to be washed and dried before they are chopped (or minced).

1. Use your fingers to remove leaves from stems; discard stems.

2. Gather leaves in small pile. Place one hand on handle of chef's knife and rest fingers of your other hand on top of blade. Use rocking motion, pivoting knife as you chop.

HOW TO CHOP ONIONS OR SHALLOTS

Shallots are smaller, milder cousins to onions. If working with a small shallot, there's no need to cut it in half.

1. Halve onion through root end, then use your fingers to remove peel. Trim top of onion.

2. Place onion half flat side down. Starting 1 inch from root end, make several vertical cuts.

3. Rotate onion and slice across first cuts. As you slice, onion will fall apart into chopped pieces.

HOW TO GRATE OR SHRED CHEESE

Cheese is often cut into very small pieces to flavor pasta, egg dishes, quesadillas, and more. When grating or shredding, use a big piece of cheese so your hand stays safely away from the sharp holes.

1. To grate: Hard cheeses like Parmesan can be rubbed against a rasp grater or the small holes of a box grater to make a fluffy pile of cheese.

2. To shred: Semisoft cheeses like cheddar or mozzarella can be rubbed against the large holes of a box grater to make long pieces of cheese.

HOW TO ZEST AND JUICE CITRUS FRUIT

The flavorful colored skin from lemons, limes, and oranges (called the zest) is often removed and used in recipes. If you need zest, it's best to zest before juicing. Once juiced, use a small spoon to remove any seeds from the bowl of juice.

1. To zest: Rub fruit against rasp grater to remove colored zest. Turn fruit as you go to avoid bitter white layer underneath zest.

2. To juice: Cut fruit in half through equator (not through ends).

3. Place 1 half of fruit in citrus juicer. Hold juicer over bowl and squeeze to extract juice.

THE ART OF GARNISHING

Garnishing is the final step that elevates your food. Keep these three plating principles in mind and see the example below. And make sure to choose garnishes that add a contrasting flavor or texture.

Patterns: Food is art and design. Adding a spiral of yogurt to soup (see below) or glittery shape to cupcakes (page 182) are great examples.

Color: Food that's a single color looks boring. Jazz up your cooking with a sprinkle of fresh herbs or bright green avocado sauce (page 126).

Symmetry: Use a light and even hand when garnishing. A big pile of minced herbs is far less attractive than a light scattering of leaves across the food.

BECOME A PLATING PRO

Gingery Carrot Soup (page 96) is the perfect blank canvas to practice your garnishing skills. Mix three parts plain yogurt with one part milk to make a creamy sauce with the right consistency for drizzling. Use a squeeze bottle (super fancy) or small spoon (as shown). Sprinkle with minced cilantro. Then finish with a few croutons.

Plain soup is so boring.

Drizzle a creamy pattern.

Hold hand high to ensure even coverage.

Artfully arrange larger garnishes.

TOOLS MAKE THE WORK EASIER

The right gear is essential. You can't cook a pound of pasta in a 2-quart saucepan. Here are the tools you will use over and over again. We've divided items into six categories: knives, cookware, kitchen basics, small appliances, prep tools, and cooking tools. You will need some specialty items, such as a muffin tin or waffle iron, for select recipes.

KNIVES

Paring knife

Chef's knife, kid-friendly (see page 121)

Cutting board

→ COOKWARE ←

Skillets, nonstick
(12-inch and 10-inch)

Skillet, traditional metal
(12-inch)

Large saucepan
(3 to 4 quarts)

Dutch oven (6 to 7 quarts)

Rimmed baking sheet

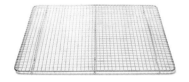

Cooling rack

KITCHEN BASICS

Prep bowls
(large, medium, small)

Oven mitts
(see page 87)

Dish towels

Paper towels

Aluminum foil

Plastic wrap

SMALL APPLIANCES

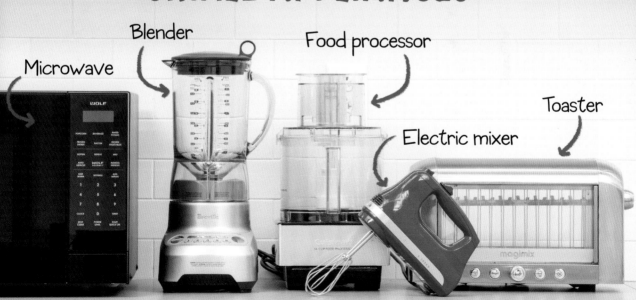

Microwave

Blender

Food processor

Electric mixer

Toaster

PREP TOOLS

Box grater

Liquid measuring cup

Dry measuring cups

Ruler

Vegetable peeler
(see page 105)

Can opener

Measuring spoons

Garlic press

Rasp grater

Citrus juicer

Salad spinner

COOKING TOOLS

Instant-read thermometer (see page 117)

Wooden spoon

Tongs

Fine-mesh strainer

Potato masher

Ladle

Spatula

Colander

Pastry brush

Whisk

Rubber spatula

Want to learn more about essential kitchen equipment and read independent product reviews?

Go to www.americastestkitchen.com/kids.

START COOKING!

1. In medium bowl, whisk together flour, sugar, baking powder, baking soda, and salt. In small bowl, whisk milk, egg, oil, and vanilla until well combined.

2. Add milk mixture to flour mixture and stir gently with rubber spatula until just combined (batter should remain lumpy). Let batter sit for 10 minutes before cooking.

3. Spray 12-inch nonstick skillet with vegetable oil spray and heat over medium heat until hot, about 1 minute.

4. Use ¼-cup dry measuring cup to scoop ¼ cup batter into skillet. Repeat 2 more times, leaving space between mounds of batter (you want 3 pancakes to cook up separate from one another).

5. Sprinkle each pancake with 1 tablespoon blueberries. Cook until bubbles on surface begin to pop, 2 to 3 minutes.

6. Use spatula to flip pancakes and cook until golden brown, 1 to 2 minutes. Transfer pancakes to plate. Repeat with remaining batter in 2 more batches. Turn off heat. Serve.

MAKE IT YOUR WAY

Pancakes are a blank canvas, so bring out your inner artist. You can work your magic at the table with **maple syrup, honey, confectioners' sugar, cinnamon sugar, fresh fruit,** and/or **softened butter**. Or you can cook your artistry right into the pancakes by adding **chocolate chips, chopped nuts, shredded coconut, sliced bananas,** or **raspberries** instead of the blueberries. Use 1 tablespoon of add-ins per pancake. Have fun and try your own combinations.

"Easy to follow, and it smelled really good. Tasted really good, and the surplus of butter made the edges crunchy."
—Zoe, 13

"Awesome!"
—Audrey, 9

FRENCH TOAST FOR ONE

SERVES 1
PREP TIME: 10 MINUTES
COOK TIME: 15 MINUTES

PREPARE INGREDIENTS

2 large slices hearty sandwich bread
½ cup milk
1 tablespoon unsalted butter, cut in half
1 large egg yolk (see page 12 for how to separate eggs)
1 tablespoon packed brown sugar
1 teaspoon vanilla extract
⅛ teaspoon ground cinnamon
Pinch salt

GATHER COOKING EQUIPMENT

Toaster
Medium microwave-safe bowl
Whisk
Pie plate or small baking dish
Spatula
2 plates
12-inch nonstick skillet

START WITH THE RIGHT BREAD

Drying out the bread in the toaster allows it to soak up the egg mixture. Don't skip this step—you want the bread to be dry and firm but not really browned. And make sure to use hearty sandwich bread—small, squishy slices can't hold as much of the eggy custard. You can use white or whole wheat bread.

START COOKING! ←—≪≪≪

1. Place bread in toaster on lowest setting. Toast until bread feels dried out and is very light brown. (You may have to toast it twice.)

2. Place milk and 1 piece of butter in medium microwave-safe bowl. Heat in microwave until butter is melted and milk is warm, 30 seconds to 1 minute.

3. Add egg yolk, sugar, vanilla, cinnamon, and salt to bowl with milk mixture and whisk to combine. Transfer mixture to pie plate or small baking dish.

4. Soak first side of 1 bread slice in milk mixture until it is wet but not falling apart, 20 seconds. Flip bread and soak second side for 20 seconds. Use spatula to remove bread from milk mixture, letting extra liquid drip back into dish. Transfer soaked bread to plate and repeat with remaining bread slice.

5. Melt remaining piece of butter in 12-inch nonstick skillet over medium-low heat. Use spatula to transfer bread slices to skillet. Cook until golden on first side, 3 to 4 minutes. Wipe spatula clean, flip slices, and cook until golden on second side, 3 to 4 minutes. Turn off heat. Transfer french toast to clean plate. Serve with maple syrup, confectioners' sugar, cinnamon sugar, butter, and/or fresh fruit.

FRENCH TOAST FOR TWO

To make french toast for two people, double all the ingredients and cook the third and fourth slices of bread after the first two slices are done. Add another ½ tablespoon of butter to the empty skillet in between the first and second batch.

OVERNIGHT WAFFLES

SERVES 4 (MAKES 7 ROUND OR 4 LARGE SQUARE WAFFLES)
PREP TIME: 15 MINUTES, PLUS OVERNIGHT RISING TIME
COOK TIME: 15 MINUTES

PREPARE INGREDIENTS

1¾ cups milk
4 tablespoons unsalted butter,
    cut into 4 pieces
2 cups all-purpose flour
1 tablespoon sugar
1½ teaspoons instant or rapid-
    rise yeast
1 teaspoon salt
2 large eggs
1 teaspoon vanilla extract

GATHER COOKING EQUIPMENT

3 bowls (1 medium microwave-safe,
    1 large, 1 small)
Rubber spatula
Whisk
Plastic wrap
Waffle iron
Dry measuring cup
Fork
Plate

"It was easy, fun, and delicious." —Kara, 10

START COOKING!

1. Place milk and butter in medium microwave-safe bowl. Cover bowl and heat in microwave for 1 minute. Stir mixture with rubber spatula. Continue to heat in microwave until butter is melted and milk is warm, 1 to 2 minutes. Let milk mixture cool, uncovered, until just warm, about 5 minutes.

2. In large bowl, whisk together flour, sugar, yeast, and salt.

3. In small bowl, whisk eggs and vanilla until combined. Slowly whisk warm milk mixture into flour mixture until smooth, then whisk in egg mixture.

4. Scrape down bowl with rubber spatula. Cover bowl tightly with plastic wrap and refrigerate for at least 12 hours or up to 24 hours.

5. Heat waffle iron. When waffle iron is hot, remove batter from refrigerator and discard plastic. Whisk batter to recombine (batter will deflate).

6. Use dry measuring cup to pour batter into middle of waffle iron. (Use about ½ cup batter for 7-inch round waffle iron or about 1 cup batter for 9-inch square waffle iron.) Close waffle iron and cook until waffle is golden brown.

7. Use fork to remove waffle from waffle iron and transfer it to plate. Repeat with remaining batter. Serve waffles with maple syrup, honey, cinnamon sugar, confectioners' sugar, whipped cream, berries, and/or softened butter.

RAISING THE BAR ↑ ON WAFFLES ↑

Overnight waffles (also known as raised or yeasted waffles) are very old-school. They do require advance planning, but they are the crispiest, tastiest waffles on the planet. They are very light and airy because they contain yeast—the magic ingredient that makes bread rise. Make the batter before bed (or even earlier in the day). When you wake up the next morning, all you have to do is heat the waffle iron, pour in the batter, and enjoy.

You can freeze any leftover waffles for one month. Stack cooled waffles with parchment or wax paper between them and then put the stack of waffles in a zipper-lock bag. Heat waffles one at a time in toaster on its lowest setting until warmed through and crisp on the outside.

KEEP IT HOT

When making waffles, pancakes, or french toast for a crowd, it can be nice to serve everything at once. If you don't, you end up being the cook while everyone else eats. To keep early batches warm, preheat your oven to 200 degrees—just warm enough to keep them hot but not so warm that they will dry out. As you make the waffles (or pancakes or french toast), place them on a cooling rack set in a rimmed baking sheet. Then place the baking sheet in the warm oven. Waffles, pancakes, and french toast can stay in the oven for 15 minutes—long enough for you to cook the remaining batches.

GRANOLA BARS

MAKES 16 BARS
PREP TIME: 20 MINUTES
COOK TIME: 1 HOUR 30 MINUTES,
    PLUS COOLING TIME

PREPARE INGREDIENTS

Vegetable oil spray
½ cup plus 1½ cups
    old-fashioned rolled oats,
    measured separately
    (no substitutions)
½ cup pecans
½ cup packed light brown sugar
3 large egg whites (see page 12
    for how to separate eggs)
⅓ cup vegetable oil
1 tablespoon vanilla extract
¼ teaspoon salt
¼ teaspoon ground cinnamon
Pinch ground nutmeg
½ cup dried cherries
½ cup raw pepitas
½ cup raw sunflower seeds
½ cup unsweetened flaked
    coconut

"Tasty, and my younger sister loved it.
I plan to make it again for my b-day party,
just without the nuts." —Zoe, 9

"I have been having these bars every day at school
for a yummy snack!" —Catherine, 10

GATHER COOKING EQUIPMENT

13-by-9-inch metal baking pan
Aluminum foil
Ruler
Food processor
2 bowls (1 small, 1 large)

Whisk
Rubber spatula
Large metal spatula
Oven mitts
Cooling rack

Cutting board
Chef's knife
Rimmed baking sheet

START COOKING! ←≪≪≪

1. Adjust oven rack to middle position and heat oven to 300 degrees. Make aluminum foil sling for 13-by-9-inch baking pan (see photos, page 172) and spray foil lightly with vegetable oil spray.

2. Add ½ cup oats to food processor and lock lid into place. Process oats until finely ground, about 30 seconds. Stop food processor. Carefully remove blade (ask an adult for help). Transfer ground oats to small bowl. Fit blade back into food processor.

3. Add pecans to now-empty food processor, lock lid back into place, and pulse until finely chopped, 5 to 8 pulses. Add pecans to bowl with ground oats.

4. In large bowl, whisk sugar, egg whites, oil, vanilla, salt, cinnamon, and nutmeg until combined. Add chopped pecans, ground oats, remaining 1½ cups whole oats, dried cherries, pepitas, sunflower seeds, and coconut and use rubber spatula to stir until well combined.

5. Transfer oat mixture to baking pan and spread into even layer. Spray bottom of large metal spatula lightly with vegetable oil spray. Use greased spatula to press firmly on top of oat mixture until mixture is very flat.

6. Place pan in oven and bake bars until light golden brown, about 40 minutes. Use oven mitts to remove pan from oven (ask an adult for help). Place pan on cooling rack and let bars cool in pan for 15 minutes; do not turn off oven.

7. Use foil to lift bars out of pan and transfer to cutting board. Use chef's knife to cut in half lengthwise. Then cut each half crosswise into 8 bars (for a total of 16 bars).

8. Line rimmed baking sheet with clean piece of foil and spray with vegetable oil spray. Space bars evenly on baking sheet and place baking sheet in oven. Bake until bars are deep golden brown, 15 to 20 minutes.

9. Use oven mitts to remove baking sheet from oven (ask an adult for help). Place baking sheet on cooling rack and let bars cool completely, about 1 hour. Serve. (Extra bars can be wrapped individually in plastic wrap and stored in zipper-lock bag or airtight container for 1 week. Bars will get softer and chewier over time.)

MAKE IT YOUR WAY

To change up the flavor in granola bars, pick a different stir-in instead of the dried cherries to add with the nuts and seeds. Have fun and try your own combinations. Use ½ cup **mini chocolate chips**, **chopped dried apricots**, or **dried cranberries**. You can also try using ½ cup **almonds** or **walnuts** instead of the pecans.

"Nice vivid and summery color. My family couldn't believe this smoothie was made by a kid." —Sophie, 10

"Making the recipe was fun. It tasted very good." —Audrey, 8

"It was very yummy. Mommy would like less honey." —Elaine, 11

STRAWBERRY-PEACH SMOOTHIES

SERVES 2
PREP TIME: 10 MINUTES
COOK TIME: 2 MINUTES

PREPARE INGREDIENTS

1 ripe banana, peeled and broken into 4 pieces
1 tablespoon honey
1 cup frozen strawberries
1 cup frozen peaches
1 cup plain yogurt
¼ cup orange juice

GATHER COOKING EQUIPMENT

Blender
Dish towel
Rubber spatula
2 glasses

START COOKING!

1. Place banana and honey in blender. Put lid on top of blender and hold firmly in place with folded dish towel (see page 95). Process until smooth, about 10 seconds.

2. Stop blender. Add strawberries, peaches, yogurt, and orange juice. Replace lid and process for 30 seconds. Stop blender and scrape down sides of blender jar with rubber spatula. Replace lid and continue to process until smooth, about 30 seconds longer. Pour into glasses and serve.

MAKE IT YOUR WAY

Once you master smoothie basics, the combinations are endless. Frozen fruit keeps things cold. If you have fresh fruit, place it in the freezer before you go to bed—voilà, frozen fruit. And follow these blender tips: ask an adult for help, never operate a blender without the lid in place (no one wants smoothie on the ceiling), and hold the lid down with a dish towel.

CHERRY-ALMOND SMOOTHIES

Add ¼ cup almond butter with banana and honey. Use 2 cups frozen cherries instead of strawberries and peaches. Use ¼ cup milk instead of orange juice.

TROPICAL FRUIT SMOOTHIES

Use 1 cup frozen mango chunks and 1 cup frozen pineapple chunks instead of strawberries and peaches. Use ¼ cup pineapple juice instead of orange juice.

MIXED BERRY SMOOTHIES

Use 2 cups frozen mixed berries instead of strawberries and peaches.

KALE-PINEAPPLE SMOOTHIES

Use 1 cup frozen pineapple chunks and 1 cup frozen chopped kale instead of strawberries and peaches.

SQUEEZE YOUR OWN OJ

Fresh-squeezed orange juice is fun to make and delicious. Some "rules" for proper squeezing:

• Use juice oranges (sometimes labeled "Valencia oranges"). Big navel oranges actually have less juice in them; the same goes for those cute little clementines.

• Cut the oranges in half. If you think of an orange as the earth, imagine the two knobby ends are the poles. When juicing an orange, cut it through the equator (the middle)—this exposes the flesh better, so you can squeeze out more juice.

• If you have a citrus juicer (a plastic jug with a reamer and a strainer to remove seeds), place one orange half on the reamer—the ridged part that squeezes the juice—and twist.

• If you're doing this by hand, get ready to build some muscles. Place a small fine-mesh strainer over a big measuring cup (for easy pouring). Squeeze the orange halves right over the strainer, which will trap seeds and some of the pulp.

• Two oranges make about one glass of juice. Do the math. If you want enough juice for four people, you will need eight oranges.

YOGURT AND BERRY PARFAITS

SERVES 2
PREP TIME: 5 MINUTES
COOK TIME: 10 MINUTES

PREPARE INGREDIENTS

1 cup plain Greek yogurt
1 tablespoon honey
1 cup raspberries, blueberries,
    blackberries, and/or sliced
    strawberries
½ cup granola

GATHER COOKING EQUIPMENT

Small bowl
Whisk
Two 8-ounce glass tumblers
¼-cup dry measuring cup
1-tablespoon measuring spoon

START COOKING! ←─≪≪≪

1. In small bowl, whisk yogurt and honey until smooth. Spoon one-quarter of the yogurt-honey mixture into each glass. Top with ¼ cup berries, followed by 2 tablespoons granola.

2. Repeat layering process with remaining yogurt, berries, and granola. When you're done, you should have 2 layers of yogurt, berries, and granola. Serve within 15 minutes or granola will start to become soggy.

"The best yogurt ever. Fun to prepare." —Jad, 9

THE LAYERED LOOK

It's easiest to complete each step in both glasses, rather than make one complete parfait and then the second one. Why? Filling both glasses at the same time helps you divide everything evenly.

Layer yogurt, berries, and granola into each glass. Repeat with more yogurt, berries, and granola.

IT'S GREEK TO ME

Creamy Greek yogurt, fresh fruit, and crunchy granola make a delicious and wholesome start to the day or a great afternoon snack—and layering them in a glass makes this simple combination feel like a special occasion. Greek yogurt makes the creamiest parfait, but there's no rule against using another kind of yogurt. You can use regular yogurt, but since it is thinner than Greek yogurt (extra liquid has been drained from Greek yogurt so that it's really thick and creamy), the layers may not stay as well defined. We like the color contrast between plain (unflavored) yogurt and the fruit, but if you use sweetened or flavored yogurt, skip the honey.

EASY FRUIT SALADS

Fruit is a great way start the day. For a special breakfast, you might want to make fruit salad. (Don't worry—no lettuce needed.) A fruit salad is a mixture of several kinds of fruit, each cut into bite-size pieces. It's nice to sweeten the fruit with a drizzle of honey or even good maple syrup. But don't use more than a drizzle—the fruit is already plenty sweet. Toss the fruit to make sure it's evenly coated with the honey. The honey will even prevent the fruit from turning brown. The best fruit salad has two or three kinds of fruit. Berries require little or no prep, and precut melon and pineapple are great choices.

Eggs might just be the most versatile ingredient in your kitchen. They can be cooked countless ways and turn up in recipes as diverse as cakes, casseroles, fresh pasta, and even ice cream. Since eggs are so quick to cook and so nutritious, every aspiring chef should learn several basic ways to cook them.

HARD-COOKED 🧑‍🍳 🍳

This is the simplest way to cook an egg. The recipe calls for just 1 ingredient: eggs (plus water). Steaming cold eggs in a steamer basket helps set the egg white proteins and ensures hard-cooked eggs that are easy to peel. Ask an adult for help with getting the eggs in and out of the saucepan.

1. Fill medium saucepan 1 inch deep with water. Bring water to rolling boil (lots of big bubbles break surface of water) over high heat.

4. While eggs are cooking, combine 2 cups ice cubes and 2 cups cold water in medium bowl.

2. Place 1 to 6 large eggs in steamer basket and carefully lower basket into saucepan. Eggs can be above or partly under water.

5. Use slotted spoon to transfer cooked eggs to ice bath; let sit for 15 minutes.

3. Cover saucepan, reduce heat to medium-low, and cook eggs for exactly 13 minutes.

6. Remove eggs from ice bath and refrigerate until ready to eat. Crack eggs against hard surface (like a counter) and peel away shell with your hands.

FRIED

Crispy fried eggs are delicious on their own or served over toast or a toasted English muffin.

1. In 10-inch nonstick skillet, heat 1 teaspoon vegetable oil over low heat for 5 minutes.

2. Meanwhile, crack 2 large eggs into small bowl and add pinch salt and pinch pepper.

3. Increase heat to medium-high and heat oil for 1 minute (oil should be hot but not smoking).

4. Working quickly, pour eggs into skillet, cover skillet, and cook for 1 minute.

5. Turn off heat and slide skillet to cool burner. Let sit, covered, for about 1 minute for slightly runny yolks or about 2 minutes for set yolks.

6. Use spatula to transfer eggs onto plate and eat immediately.

SCRAMBLED

The extra yolk and half-and-half ensure that your scrambled eggs are tender, not tough.

1. Crack 3 large eggs into medium bowl. Crack 1 large egg, separate yolk from white, and discard white. Place yolk in bowl with whole eggs.

2. Add 1 tablespoon half-and-half or whole milk along with pinch salt and pinch pepper. Whisk until well combined and uniform yellow color.

3. In 10-inch nonstick skillet, melt 1 tablespoon butter over medium heat until hot, swirling to evenly coat skillet, about 1 minute.

4. Add eggs to pan. Stir with spatula until eggs have clumped and are still slightly wet, 1 to 2 minutes. (Scrape bottom of skillet several times as eggs cook.) Turn off heat. Transfer eggs to plate and eat immediately.

> "I don't like avocado, but with eggs and bread, it was good."
> —Andrew, 9

AVOCADO TOAST WITH FRIED EGGS

SERVES 2
PREP TIME: 10 MINUTES
COOK TIME: 15 MINUTES

PREPARE INGREDIENTS

1 tablespoon plus 2 teaspoons extra-virgin olive oil, measured separately
1 teaspoon lemon juice, squeezed from ½ lemon
Salt and pepper
1 ripe avocado
2 (½-inch-thick) slices crusty bread
2 large eggs

GATHER COOKING EQUIPMENT

2 small bowls
Whisk
Cutting board
Butter knife
Soupspoon
Fork
Toaster
10-inch nonstick skillet with lid
Spatula

→ THE "IT" TOAST ←

Some dishes are so simple that they are not even worth talking about. But avocado toast deserves a shout-out; it's healthy and delicious, and it's one of the simplest things to make for a quick snack. With the avocado mixture smeared on toasted crusty bread, this dish is spectacularly tasty. Adding a fried egg takes it over the top and turns this hearty snack into a great breakfast or lunch. Of course, you can skip the egg and just enjoy the avocado and toast.

FEAR NOT THE AVOCADO

Avocados are so yummy, but they can be tricky to work with. We suggest asking an adult to help until you master this method.

1. Use butter knife to cut avocado in half lengthwise around pit.

2. Using your hands, twist both halves in opposite directions to separate.

3. Use soupspoon to scoop out pit; discard pit.

4. Use spoon to scoop out avocado from skin; discard skin. Avocado can now be sliced, chopped, or mashed.

"Surprisingly, I thought it was good." —Ronan, 9

START COOKING!

"Impressed my brother, who is an athlete." —Benedict, 10

1. In small bowl, whisk together 1 tablespoon oil, lemon juice, pinch salt, and pinch pepper.

2. Use butter knife to cut avocado in half (see photos, above). Separate halves, then remove and discard pit. Scoop avocado into bowl with lemon dressing; discard skin. Use fork to break avocado into large pieces, then mash into dressing until mostly smooth.

3. Place bread in toaster and toast until golden on both sides, 1 to 2 minutes. Spread avocado mixture evenly on toasts.

4. In 10-inch nonstick skillet, heat remaining 2 teaspoons oil over low heat for 5 minutes. Meanwhile, crack eggs into second small bowl and add pinch salt and pinch pepper.

5. Increase heat to medium-high and heat oil for 1 minute (oil should be hot but not smoking). Working quickly, pour eggs into skillet, cover skillet, and cook for 1 minute.

6. Turn off heat and slide skillet to cool burner. Let sit, covered, for about 1 minute for slightly runny yolks or about 2 minutes for set yolks.

7. Use spatula to transfer 1 fried egg to each toast. Serve.

BREAKFAST TACOS WITH BACON

SERVES 2 TO 4
PREP TIME: 20 MINUTES
COOK TIME: 15 MINUTES

PREPARE INGREDIENTS

4 large eggs
⅛ teaspoon salt
Pinch pepper
1 slice bacon, cut into ½-inch pieces
1 scallion, sliced thin
4 (6-inch) flour or corn tortillas
½ cup tomato salsa (jarred or homemade, see page 58)
¼ cup shredded Monterey Jack cheese
1 lime, cut into wedges

GATHER COOKING EQUIPMENT

Medium bowl
Whisk
10-inch nonstick skillet
Rubber spatula
Microwave-safe plate
Dish towel

"Eggs and bacon together are so good."
—Lawman, 9

"I want to make these for my birthday."
—Harper, 10

START COOKING! ←〈〈〈〈

1. In medium bowl, whisk eggs, salt, and pepper until well combined and uniform yellow color, about 1 minute. Set aside.

2. In 10-inch nonstick skillet, cook bacon over medium heat, stirring occasionally with rubber spatula until crispy, about 4 minutes.

3. Stir scallion into skillet and cook until just softened, about 1 minute.

4. Add eggs to skillet and gently stir, scraping bottom of skillet, until eggs have clumped and are still slightly wet, 1 to 2 minutes. Turn off heat and slide skillet to cool burner.

5. Stack tortillas on microwave-safe plate, cover with damp dish towel, and heat in microwave until warm, about 20 seconds.

6. Divide egg mixture evenly among warm tortillas. Serve with salsa, cheese, and lime wedges.

TWO WAYS TO COOK BACON

To ensure that your bacon cooks up extra crispy, try one of these methods.

OVEN

This is the best way to cook bacon for a crowd, but you will need help from an adult.

Adjust oven rack to middle position and heat oven to 400 degrees. Line rimmed baking sheet with aluminum foil. Arrange strips of bacon (as much as 1 pound) on foil (slices can overlap slightly). Place baking sheet in oven and bake until bacon is browned and crispy, 10 to 15 minutes. Baking sheet (and grease) will be very hot! Ask an adult to remove baking sheet from oven. Carefully transfer bacon to plate lined with paper towels to drain.

STOVETOP

The water reduces splattering and ensures that bacon doesn't scorch before all the fat is cooked off.

Place 4 strips of bacon in 12-inch skillet (regular or nonstick) and add ½ cup water. Turn heat to high. When water comes to boil, reduce heat to medium and continue cooking until water evaporates, about 5 minutes. Reduce heat to medium-low and keep cooking until bacon is crispy and golden brown on first side, about 2 minutes. Use tongs to flip bacon and cook until crispy and golden brown on second side, about 2 minutes. Transfer bacon to plate lined with paper towels to drain.

"Should have made another."
—Lawman, 9

CHEESE OMELET

SERVES 1
PREP TIME: 5 MINUTES
COOK TIME: 5 MINUTES

PREPARE INGREDIENTS

2 large eggs
Pinch salt
Pinch pepper
1 tablespoon unsalted butter
2 tablespoons shredded
   cheddar cheese

GATHER COOKING EQUIPMENT

Medium bowl
Whisk
10-inch nonstick skillet
Rubber spatula
Plate

START COOKING!

1. In medium bowl, whisk eggs, salt, and pepper until well combined.

2. In 10-inch nonstick skillet, melt butter over medium heat until hot, swirling to evenly coat skillet, about 1 minute.

3. Add eggs to skillet and stir gently with rubber spatula until eggs just begin to set, about 10 seconds.

4. Use spatula to gently pull and lift cooked eggs into center of skillet (see photos, right). Tilt and swirl skillet so uncooked eggs run to cleared edges of skillet. Cook until egg on top is mostly set but still moist, 1 to 2 minutes.

5. Turn off heat. Sprinkle omelet with cheese and let melt, about 20 seconds. Use rubber spatula to carefully fold omelet in half, forming half-moon shape with cheese inside. Slide omelet onto plate and serve.

MAKE IT YOUR WAY

In addition to substituting your favorite cheese for the cheddar, you can customize your omelet with add-ins (use one or make your own combo): **quartered cherry tomatoes, diced ham, chopped baby spinach, chopped scallions, minced chives,** or **minced parsley.** Sprinkle 2 tablespoons of your favorite add-in ingredients over half of omelet after you sprinkle with cheese.

MASTER CHEF, THE OMELET COMPETITION

Making a good omelet is about watching the skillet and using the right wrist action. Don't try this recipe unless you have a nonstick skillet.

1. Once eggs begin to set, use spatula to gently pull and lift cooked eggs into center of skillet. Tilt and swirl skillet so uncooked eggs run to cleared edges of skillet.

2. Once cheese has melted, use rubber spatula to carefully fold omelet in half, forming half-moon shape with cheese inside.

THE FRENCH KNOW EGGS

A nicely cooked omelet is a thing of beauty. Some well-known French restaurant chefs like to evaluate potential new kitchen hires by asking them to make an omelet. It seems so simple, but it's not easy. Practice often and you will get the hang of it! This recipe is best done with adult supervision.

"Looks like they don't have a lot of berries from outside, but there are a lot."
—Charlotte, 13

"Don't need to buy muffins again!"
—Teo, 9

BLUEBERRY MUFFINS

MAKES 12 MUFFINS
PREP TIME: 15 MINUTES
COOK TIME: 40 MINUTES, PLUS COOLING TIME

PREPARE INGREDIENTS

Vegetable oil spray
3 cups plus 1 tablespoon all-purpose flour, measured separately
1 cup sugar
1 tablespoon baking powder
½ teaspoon baking soda
½ teaspoon salt
1½ cups plain yogurt
2 large eggs
8 tablespoons unsalted butter, melted and cooled (see page 12 for how to melt butter)
1½ cups fresh or frozen blueberries (do not thaw if frozen)

GATHER COOKING EQUIPMENT

12-cup muffin tin
3 bowls (1 large, 1 medium, 1 small)
Whisk
Rubber spatula
⅓-cup dry measuring cup
Toothpick
Oven mitts
Cooling rack

START COOKING!

1. Adjust oven rack to middle position and heat oven to 375 degrees. Spray 12-cup muffin tin with vegetable oil spray.

2. In large bowl, whisk together 3 cups flour, sugar, baking powder, baking soda, and salt. In medium bowl, whisk yogurt and eggs until smooth.

3. Add yogurt mixture to flour mixture and use rubber spatula to stir gently until just combined and no dry flour is visible. Gently stir in melted butter.

4. In small bowl, toss blueberries with remaining 1 tablespoon flour. Gently stir blueberries into batter. Do not overmix.

5. Use ⅓-cup dry measuring cup to divide batter evenly among muffin cups (use rubber spatula to scrape batter from cups if needed).

6. Place muffin tin in oven and bake until golden brown and toothpick inserted in center of muffin comes out clean (see photo, page 173), 20 to 25 minutes.

7. Use oven mitts to remove muffin tin from oven (ask an adult to help). Place muffin tin on cooling rack and let muffins cool in tin for 15 minutes.

8. Using your fingertips, gently wiggle muffins to loosen from muffin tin and transfer to cooling rack. Let cool for at least 10 minutes before serving.

MAKE IT YOUR WAY

There are many reasons to love muffins. First off, you're basically eating cake for breakfast. Second, you can stir in almost anything to make muffins just the way you like them. Here are some of our favorite ideas. Tossing the blueberries with a little flour keeps their color from bleeding into the muffins. Unless you like purple muffins, don't skip this step. However, you can skip the flouring step if using other fruit: only blueberries bleed.

BANANA-WALNUT MUFFINS

Use 1 cup packed light brown sugar instead of sugar. Use 1½ cups finely chopped bananas and ½ cup coarsely chopped walnuts instead of blueberries.

CHERRY-ALMOND MUFFINS

Use 1½ cups dried cherries instead of blueberries. Once muffin batter is in muffin tin, sprinkle batter with ¼ cup sliced almonds before baking.

CHOCOLATE CHIP MUFFINS

Use 1 cup chocolate chips instead of blueberries.

MONKEY BREAD

SERVES 8
PREP TIME: 10 MINUTES
COOK TIME: 2 TO 3 HOURS

PREPARE INGREDIENTS

½ cup packed light brown sugar
1½ teaspoons ground cinnamon
⅛ teaspoon ground nutmeg
6 tablespoons unsalted butter,
  melted and cooled (see page
  12 for how to melt butter)
Vegetable oil spray
1 pound pizza dough, room
  temperature (store-bought
  or see page 136 to make
  your own)
⅓ cup confectioners' sugar
2 teaspoons milk

GATHER COOKING EQUIPMENT

3 small bowls
8-inch round cake pan
Ruler
Kitchen shears
Plastic wrap
Oven mitts
Cooling rack
Large plate
Spoon

"Absolutely amazing!"—Nate, 8

"Really fun to make." —Andrea, 12, & Julia, 12

START COOKING! ←※※※

1. In small bowl, stir together brown sugar, cinnamon, and nutmeg. Place melted butter in second small bowl. Spray 8-inch round cake pan with vegetable oil spray.

2. Spray counter lightly with vegetable oil spray. Place dough on greased counter and pat into 6-inch square. Use kitchen shears to cut dough into 36 pieces (see photos, right).

3. Roll each piece of dough into ball. Dip each ball in melted butter to coat, roll in brown sugar mixture, then place in greased pan. Cover bottom of pan with dough balls in single layer.

4. Cover pan tightly with plastic wrap and leave in warm place until dough balls are puffy and have risen slightly (about ½ inch), 1 to 2 hours.

5. Adjust oven rack to middle position and heat oven to 350 degrees. Discard plastic. Place pan in oven and bake until top of monkey bread is light golden brown, 20 to 25 minutes.

6. Use oven mitts to remove monkey bread from oven (ask an adult to help). Place pan on cooling rack and let monkey bread cool for 5 minutes (no longer).

7. Place large plate on top of pan. Ask an adult to carefully flip out monkey bread onto plate. Remove pan. Let cool for 10 minutes before glazing.

8. In third small bowl, stir confectioners' sugar and milk until smooth. Use spoon to drizzle glaze over monkey bread. Serve warm.

MONKEY BREAD is a knotty-looking loaf of sweet bread made from balls of dough coated with cinnamon, sugar, and melted butter. It's traditionally served warm so that the sticky baked pieces can be pulled apart. The name "monkey" refers to how you eat this sweet treat—with your hands.

1. Pat dough into 6-inch square. Use kitchen shears to cut dough in half. Cut each half into 3 strips (you'll have 6 strips total). Cut each strip into 6 even pieces (you'll have 36 pieces total).

2. Roll each piece of dough into ball. Dip each ball in melted butter to coat, roll in brown sugar mixture, then place in greased cake pan.

3. Let baked monkey bread cool in pan on cooling rack for 5 minutes, then place large plate on top of pan. Ask an adult to flip out monkey bread onto plate. Wearing oven mitts, remove pan. Let cool for 10 minutes before glazing.

"A tasty meal for the whole family." —Talia, 9

OVERNIGHT OATMEAL WITH RAISINS AND BROWN SUGAR

SERVES 4
PREP TIME: 10 MINUTES,
   PLUS OVERNIGHT RESTING TIME
COOK TIME: 15 MINUTES

PREPARE INGREDIENTS

3 cups plus 1 cup water,
   measured separately
1 cup steel-cut oats
¼ teaspoon salt
½ cup raisins
3 tablespoons packed
   brown sugar
1 tablespoon unsalted butter
¼ teaspoon ground cinnamon

GATHER COOKING EQUIPMENT

Large saucepan with lid
Wooden spoon or rubber spatula

START COOKING!

1. In large saucepan, bring 3 cups water to boil over high heat. Turn off heat and slide saucepan to cool burner. Stir in oats and salt. Cover saucepan with lid and let sit overnight.

2. In morning, stir remaining 1 cup water into saucepan with oats and bring to boil over medium-high heat. Reduce heat to medium and cook, stirring occasionally, until mixture is creamy and oats are tender but chewy, 4 to 6 minutes.

3. Turn off heat and slide saucepan to cool burner. Stir in raisins, sugar, butter, and cinnamon. Cover and let sit for 5 minutes. Serve.

MAKE IT YOUR WAY

If you think oatmeal comes in a packet, think again. They know about oatmeal in Ireland and Scotland, where whole-grain, steel-cut oats are popular. Yes, these slightly chewy oats take longer to cook than old-fashioned rolled oats (and way longer than instant oats in a packet), but the results are so much better. To shorten the usual half-hour cooking time, start the process at night and then finish up in the morning. If you don't like raisins and cinnamon, try these fun flavor combinations.

BANANA AND BROWN SUGAR OATMEAL

Use 2 chopped ripe bananas instead of raisins. Leave out cinnamon.

BLUEBERRY AND ALMOND OATMEAL

Use ½ cup blueberries instead of raisins. Use 2 tablespoons almond butter instead of butter and cinnamon. Add ½ cup sliced almonds to oatmeal along with blueberries in step 3.

TOASTED COCONUT OATMEAL

In step 2, use 1 cup canned coconut milk instead of water. Use ½ cup toasted unsweetened flaked coconut instead of raisins. Leave out butter and cinnamon.

THE MASTER OF TOAST

Well-made toast completes any breakfast. It's also a great quick breakfast on its own—just add a piece of fruit. Here are some guidelines for making toast worth celebrating.

• Start with good bread. Egg-enriched challah and brioche make amazing toast—trust us. It's fine to toast slightly stale bread. Sliced bread kept in the freezer is perfect for toasting.

• Stay away from bread with big holes—a fine, even crumb (the part of the bread inside the crust) is key. Big holes mean butter or jam on your shirt!

• Cold butter doesn't spread well. Soften butter in the microwave for 5 to 10 seconds (but don't let it melt). Sprinkle the buttered toast with some cinnamon sugar, and you're all set.

• Other ideas for topping toast generally start with something sticky, such as peanut butter, hummus (try it), or honey. Next add something fruity (banana or apple slices, berries, raisins) and/or something crunchy (chopped nuts or seeds, shredded coconut, or even granola).

CHAPTER 2: SNACKS & BEVERAGES

SNACK FOOD IS FUN FOOD. LOOKING FOR AN AFTER-SCHOOL NOSH OR MAYBE SOMETHING FOR A SLEEPOVER PARTY? IT'S ALL HERE.

REAL BUTTERED POPCORN

SERVES 3 TO 4 (MAKES 6 CUPS)
PREP TIME: 5 MINUTES
COOK TIME: 10 MINUTES

PREPARE INGREDIENTS

¼ cup popcorn kernels
½ teaspoon vegetable oil
1 tablespoon unsalted butter
¼ teaspoon salt

GATHER COOKING EQUIPMENT

Clean brown paper lunch bag
Large microwave-safe plate
Oven mitts
Large microwave-safe bowl
Rubber spatula

START COOKING!

1. Place popcorn kernels in clean brown paper lunch bag. Drizzle kernels with oil. Fold over top of bag three times to seal (do not tape or staple).

2. Shake bag to coat kernels with oil, place bag on its side on large microwave-safe plate, and shake kernels into even layer in bag.

3. Place plate in microwave and cook until popping slows down to one or two pops at a time, 3 to 5 minutes. Use oven mitts to remove plate from microwave (plate will be very hot, ask an adult to help). Set aside to cool slightly.

4. Place butter in large microwave-safe bowl (big enough to hold popcorn), cover, and heat in microwave at 50 percent power until melted, 30 to 60 seconds. Use oven mitts to remove bowl from microwave.

5. Carefully open paper bag (be careful of hot steam) and pour popcorn into bowl with melted butter. Use rubber spatula to toss popcorn with butter. Sprinkle with salt. Serve.

MAKE IT YOUR WAY

Why stick with just butter and salt when it comes to popcorn flavorings? Here are some inventive ways to make popcorn special—perfect for a sleepover or a movie night with friends.

PARMESAN-HERB POPCORN

In small bowl, stir together ¼ cup grated Parmesan cheese and 1 tablespoon Italian seasoning blend. Sprinkle over popcorn along with salt just before serving.

SRIRACHA-LIME POPCORN

Stir ½ teaspoon sriracha sauce into melted butter. Sprinkle ½ teaspoon grated lime zest over popcorn along with salt just before serving.

CINNAMON-MALT POPCORN

In small bowl, stir together 1 tablespoon malted milk powder, 1 tablespoon packed brown sugar, and ½ teaspoon ground cinnamon. Sprinkle over popcorn along with salt just before serving.

DO-IT-YOURSELF MICROWAVE POPCORN

Microwave popcorn is a great idea—in theory. But most packaged options have a long list of unnatural ingredients and don't taste very good. This fun recipe turns a plain old brown paper bag—the kind you might use to hold your lunch—into a microwave-safe package for popping corn kernels. Make sure to use a plain bag without any writing (colored inks are often not microwave-safe). Microwaves vary in strength so rather than watching the clock, listen for the popping sounds: when they slow down, the popcorn is ready. Be careful when opening the bag with the popped kernels—there will be a lot of steam in the bag, so open it away from your face or hands.

"Making it was super fun.
It tasted awesome.
Two thumbs up!"
—Savannah, 9

"My sister and I made these
all by ourselves."
—Annie, 12, & Lizzy, 11

TOMATO AND MOZZARELLA BITES

SERVES 2 TO 4
PREP TIME: 5 MINUTES
COOK TIME: 10 MINUTES

PREPARE INGREDIENTS

8 grape or cherry tomatoes
8 baby mozzarella balls
1 tablespoon extra-virgin olive oil
Salt and pepper
8 fresh small basil leaves

GATHER COOKING EQUIPMENT

Paring knife
Cutting board
Medium bowl
Rubber spatula
8 sturdy wooden toothpicks, each about 3 inches long

START COOKING!

1. Cut tomatoes in half and place in medium bowl. Add mozzarella balls and drizzle with oil. Sprinkle with salt and pepper and use rubber spatula to toss gently.

2. Slide tomato half onto sturdy wooden toothpick. Slide basil leaf onto toothpick, then slide mozzarella ball onto toothpick. Finish each skewer by sliding second tomato half onto end. Serve.

GETTING TO KNOW HERBS

Fresh herbs make food look and taste better. Below are four herbs used in recipes throughout the book—along with notes on what they taste like. Some general tips:

- Many supermarkets spray herbs with water. If herbs are really wet when you get them home, wrap the bunch in paper towels, slide the rolled up herbs into a plastic bag, and then refrigerate in the crisper drawer. Leave the bag partially open so herbs don't get soggy and slimy.

- When ready to use herbs, wash and dry them in a salad spinner.

- In most cases, the stems are tough and should be discarded before the leaves are chopped (see photos, page 13).

- Planting herbs in the garden or in window pots is a great way to make sure you always have them on hand.

BASIL tastes a little like licorice with notes of orange. Italian recipes often call for basil, in everything from tomato sauces to pesto. Basil is very perishable—the leaves shrivel or blacken in just a few days—so don't buy too much at a time and don't chop until you're ready to use it.

PARSLEY adds color and grassy flavor to dishes from around the globe. There are two types of parsley—flat leaf (seen here, with dark green, flat leaves) and curly leaf (with frilly tops that are lighter in color). Flat-leaf parsley has more flavor and is the better option.

CILANTRO is used in many Mexican, Asian, and Mediterranean dishes. Its flavor is lemony and even a bit flowery. Some people find cilantro soapy-tasting. If you're in this camp, use parsley in its place. Cilantro stems are tender and flavorful, so it's fine if you chop them up with the leaves.

THYME has a woodsy, almost minty flavor that's pretty strong, so a little goes a long way. Thyme works really well with chicken, meat, and potatoes. Although delicate basil, parsley, and cilantro are typically added just before serving, thyme is quite hearty and usually cooked.

SNACK ON A SKEWER

You will need sturdy wooden toothpicks, roughly 3 inches long, for this recipe. Regular toothpicks are too short. Fresh baby mozzarella balls packed in water are tender and soak up the oil best; shrink-wrapped mozzarella (the kind you generally use on pizza) won't be as good in this recipe. Larger balls of fresh mozzarella packed in water can be cut into ¾-inch chunks if you can't find baby size. This recipe is perfect for a party, and you can double or triple all the ingredients—just make sure you have the right number of toothpicks.

"Creamy and a little chunky. But mostly creamy."
—Nate, 8

HUMMUS

SERVES 6 (MAKES ABOUT 1½ CUPS)
PREP TIME: 10 MINUTES
COOK TIME: 5 MINUTES

PREPARE INGREDIENTS

¼ cup water
2 tablespoons lemon juice, squeezed from 1 lemon
2 tablespoons tahini (stirred well before measuring)
2 tablespoons extra-virgin olive oil
1 (15-ounce) can chickpeas
1 garlic clove, peeled (see photo, page 13)
½ teaspoon salt
¼ teaspoon ground cumin

GATHER COOKING EQUIPMENT

Liquid measuring cup
Spoon
Colander
Can opener
Food processor
Rubber spatula
Small bowl

THE FOOD PROCESSOR IS YOUR FRIEND

When the food processor was introduced in the 1970s, it suddenly made difficult or time-consuming recipes so much easier. The fast blades combine ingredients in just seconds. Hummus is a perfect example—this creamy spread is made with pureed chickpeas, tahini (which is like peanut butter but is made from sesame seeds), lemon juice, and spices. Before the food processor, you had to beat these ingredients by hand. It was tough work turning chickpeas (a member of the bean family) into a smooth puree. The food processor makes hummus, and many other recipes, much easier and faster to prepare. Talk about a tasty invention.

START COOKING!

1. In liquid measuring cup, stir together water, lemon juice, tahini, and oil.

2. Set colander in sink. Open can of chickpeas and pour into colander. Rinse chickpeas with cold water and shake colander to drain well.

3. Transfer chickpeas to food processor. Add garlic, salt, and cumin to food processor and lock lid into place. Process mixture for 10 seconds.

4. Stop food processor, remove lid, and scrape down sides of bowl with rubber spatula. Lock lid back into place and process until mixture is coarsely ground, about 5 seconds.

5. With processor running, slowly pour water mixture through feed tube until mixture is smooth, about 1 minute.

6. Stop food processor. Carefully remove food processor blade (ask an adult for help). Transfer hummus to small bowl. Serve. (Leftover hummus can be refrigerated for up to 5 days. Before serving, stir in 1 tablespoon warm water to loosen hummus.)

THE DIPPING LIFE

A flavorful dip, such as hummus, is a great snack. Use baby carrots, slices of cucumber, whole cherry tomatoes, crackers, pita chips, or even Tortilla Snack Chips (page 56) as your "scooper" and you're good to go. You can also drizzle your hummus with some extra olive oil before serving for a fancy touch. Don't have a can of chickpeas in the pantry? You can turn plain yogurt, preferably thicker Greek-style yogurt, into a super fast dip. (Whatever you do, no raspberry yogurt, please!) Here are some ideas to get you started, but feel free to add flavors as you like.

GREEK YOGURT DIP

In small bowl, stir together 1 cup plain Greek yogurt, ½ cup crumbled feta cheese, 2 tablespoons chopped fresh mint, 1 teaspoon extra-virgin olive oil, and pinch salt.

FRENCH ONION YOGURT DIP

In small bowl, stir together 1 cup plain Greek yogurt, 2 tablespoons finely chopped chives, 1 tablespoon onion powder, ½ teaspoon garlic powder, and ¼ teaspoon salt.

TAHINI-LEMON YOGURT DIP

In small bowl, stir together 1 cup plain Greek yogurt, 2 tablespoons tahini, 1 tablespoon lemon juice, 1 teaspoon honey, and pinch salt.

TORTILLA SNACK CHIPS

SERVES 4
PREP TIME: 5 MINUTES
COOK TIME: 25 MINUTES

PREPARE INGREDIENTS

4 (8-inch) flour tortillas
Vegetable oil spray
½ teaspoon salt

GATHER COOKING EQUIPMENT

Cutting board
Chef's knife
Large bowl
2 rimmed baking sheets
Oven mitts
2 cooling racks

"Almost light when you bite in. Not too much salt." —Nolan, 11

"Not too crunchy. Looks really good and shiny." —Myles, 10

START COOKING!

1. Adjust oven racks to upper-middle and lower-middle positions and heat oven to 350 degrees.

2. Cut each tortilla into 8 wedges (see photos, right) and transfer to large bowl. Spray wedges generously with vegetable oil spray. Sprinkle with salt. Use your hands to gently toss tortilla pieces to make sure they are evenly coated and shiny on all sides. Use more cooking spray if needed.

3. Spread half of tortilla pieces onto rimmed baking sheet in single layer. Spread remaining tortilla pieces onto second rimmed baking sheet in single layer.

4. Place both baking sheets in oven and bake until chips are golden and crisp, 10 to 15 minutes. (Note that chips on lower rack may cook more quickly.)

5. Use oven mitts to remove baking sheets from oven (ask an adult for help). Place baking sheets on cooling racks and let chips cool for 10 minutes. Serve. (Chips can be stored in airtight container for up to 4 days.)

MAKE IT YOUR WAY

These chips are great for scooping up your favorite dip. Try them with Hummus (page 54), ranch dressing, Quick Tomato Salsa (page 58), Guacamole (page 60), or even peanut butter! They're also great to munch with a piece of cheese or a slice of fruit. You can add more character to the chips by using these flavor mixtures instead of salt. Make them all and have a party!

PIZZA CHIPS

In small bowl, combine 1 teaspoon Italian seasoning, 1 teaspoon paprika, ½ teaspoon garlic powder, and ¼ teaspoon salt. In step 2, use this mixture instead of salt.

CINNAMON-SUGAR CHIPS

In small bowl, combine 2 tablespoons granulated sugar and 1 tablespoon ground cinnamon. In step 2, use cinnamon sugar instead of salt.

RANCH CHIPS

In step 2, use 1 tablespoon packaged ranch seasoning mix instead of salt.

HOW A CIRCLE BECOMES 8 TRIANGLES

To turn flour tortillas into chips, think of each tortilla as a pizza or a pie that you cut into triangular wedges. Here's how to turn each circle into 8 triangles.

1. Cut each tortilla in half from top to bottom and then again from side to side. You should now have 4 same-size, triangle-shaped pieces.

2. Keep pieces together in circle and cut on diagonal through middles of triangles. You are cutting each large triangle in half to produce 8 smaller, equally sized triangles.

QUICK TOMATO SALSA

SERVES 4 (MAKES ABOUT 1 CUP)
PREP TIME: 10 MINUTES
COOK TIME: 10 MINUTES

PREPARE INGREDIENTS

1 (14.5-ounce) can diced tomatoes
¼ cup fresh cilantro leaves
2 slices jarred pickled jalapeños
2 teaspoons lime juice, squeezed
    from 1 lime
1 garlic clove, peeled (see photo,
    page 13)
¼ teaspoon salt

GATHER COOKING EQUIPMENT

Fine-mesh strainer
Large bowl
Can opener
Rubber spatula
Food processor
Small bowl

"I'm not a salsa lover, but I liked it." —Sophia, 13

"I thought the recipe was a good starting point but could use more flavor! Maybe more jalapeño peppers or garlic." —Celia, 12

SALSA IN THREE BEATS

If you start with canned diced tomatoes, home-made salsa comes together in the time it takes to listen to one song (salsa music or not). And because they are picked at the height of fresh-ness, canned tomatoes taste good year-round. The food processor is key to making this recipe so simple. Use whole cilantro leaves (no need to chop; just pack washed and dried leaves into a ¼-cup dry measuring cup), pickled jalapeños (use a small fork to lift them out of the brine and drain off the liquid), and freshly squeezed lime juice. If you don't like spicy salsa, leave out the jalapeños.

START COOKING!

1. Set fine-mesh strainer over large bowl. Open can of diced tomatoes and pour into fine-mesh strainer. Use rubber spatula to stir and press on tomatoes to remove liquid. Let tomatoes drain in strainer for 5 minutes.

2. Place cilantro, jalapeños, lime juice, garlic, and salt in food processor. Lock lid in place. Hold down pulse button for 1 second, then release. Repeat until ingredients are roughly chopped, about 5 pulses. Remove lid and scrape down sides of bowl.

3. Add drained tomatoes to mixture in food processor. Lock lid into place and pulse until evenly chopped, about 2 pulses. Remove lid and carefully remove food processor blade (ask an adult for help). Transfer salsa to small bowl. Serve. (Salsa can be refrigerated in airtight container for 2 days.)

GUACAMOLE

SERVES 8 (MAKES ABOUT 2 CUPS)
PREP TIME: 10 MINUTES
COOK TIME: 10 MINUTES

PREPARE INGREDIENTS

3 ripe avocados
1 lime
½ teaspoon salt
1 plum tomato, chopped
2 tablespoons chopped fresh cilantro
  (see page 13 for how to chop herbs)
1 scallion, sliced thin

GATHER COOKING EQUIPMENT

Cutting board
Butter knife
Soupspoon
Medium bowl
Rasp grater (or box grater)
¼-teaspoon measuring spoon
Chef's knife
Whisk
Rubber spatula

"Lime-y." —Clementine, 12

"I like the chunks. I normally don't." —Daphne, 13

START COOKING!

1. Use butter knife to cut avocado in half around pit (see photos, page 37). With your hands, twist both halves in opposite directions to separate. Use soupspoon to scoop out pit. Scoop avocado from skins into medium bowl; discard pits and skins.

2. Use rasp grater or fine holes on box grater to remove ¼ teaspoon zest (the colored skin) from lime (see photo, page 14). Add zest to bowl with avocados.

3. Use chef's knife to cut lime in half and squeeze juice into bowl with avocados. Add salt to bowl.

4. Use sturdy whisk to break avocado into large pieces. Gently stir mixture to combine, leaving some large chunks of avocado. Gently tap whisk on rim of bowl to remove any stuck avocado pieces and remove whisk from bowl.

5. Add tomato, cilantro, and scallion to avocado mixture and use rubber spatula to gently stir together. Serve.

AVOCADO PRIMER

Here's what to know about shopping for and storing everyone's favorite green fruit.

• Buy small, rough-skinned Hass avocados. Their rich flavor and buttery texture are essential for guacamole. Large, bright-green avocados are fine for salads but aren't rich enough for guacamole.

• While Hass avocados start out green and get progressively more purple-black as they ripen, color alone isn't an accurate indicator of ripeness.

• The most accurate test for ripeness is to place the fruit in the palm of your hand and gently squeeze: It should be a little soft.

• Storing avocados in a paper bag at room temperature will speed up ripening by trapping ethylene, the gas that triggers ripening in many fruits and vegetables.

• Unless you plan to eat them immediately, keep ripe avocados in the refrigerator, which can extend their shelf life by days.

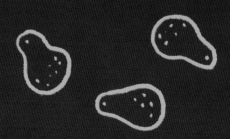

KALE CHIPS

SERVES 2
PREP TIME: 5 MINUTES
COOK TIME: 1½ HOURS

PREPARE INGREDIENTS

4 ounces Lacinato kale
1 teaspoon extra-virgin olive oil
¼ teaspoon kosher salt

GATHER COOKING EQUIPMENT

2 cooling racks
Rimmed baking sheet
Kitchen shears
Cutting board
Salad spinner
2 dish towels
Large bowl
Oven mitts

"It was easy to make! Found it took a bit longer
than an hour to get them nice and crisp."
—Kaeden, 11

"I put in a little too much salt by accident, so
next time I make it I'm going to add less salt.
Would totally make it again."
—Ocean, 10

1. Use kitchen shears to cut down each side of thick stem; discard stem.

2. Use your hands to tear dark-green leaves into large pieces, about 3 inches each.

START COOKING!

1. Adjust oven rack to middle position and heat oven to 200 degrees. Set cooling rack in rimmed baking sheet.

2. Use kitchen shears to separate stems of kale from leaves (see photos, above); discard stems. Tear leaves into 3-inch pieces (pieces can vary in size; you should have about 4 cups).

3. Wash kale in salad spinner and spin dry. Spread out kale on clean dish towel, cover with second clean dish towel, and pat dry.

4. Transfer kale to large bowl and drizzle with oil. Use your hands to rub oil onto kale until it is well coated and shiny. Spread kale out in even layer on cooling rack. Sprinkle evenly with salt.

5. Place baking sheet in oven and bake until kale chips are very crisp, 1 to 1¼ hours.

6. Use oven mitts to remove baking sheet from oven (ask an adult for help). Place baking sheet on second cooling rack. Let chips cool completely, about 10 minutes. Serve.

MAKE IT YOUR WAY

Move over, potatoes—you aren't the only vegetable that makes delicious crunchy chips. Kale chips are definitely the best way to eat this super healthy veggie. Just tear kale leaves into small pieces, toss them with olive oil, sprinkle them with salt, and then bake them in a really low-temperature oven until they're dry. Lacinato kale (also known as Tuscan or dinosaur kale) has bumpy dark green leaves and produces the best chips. Curly leaf kale, the most common variety, will work in this recipe, but baby kale won't. No matter what kind of kale you're using, make sure the leaves are completely dry. Once you master the basic recipe, try these flavored kale chips.

RANCH KALE CHIPS

In step 4, sprinkle kale with 2 teaspoons ranch seasoning mix instead of salt.

SESAME-GINGER KALE CHIPS

In step 4, use 1 teaspoon toasted sesame oil instead of olive oil. In small bowl, stir together 1 teaspoon sesame seeds and ¼ teaspoon ground ginger with salt. Sprinkle sesame-ginger mixture over kale just before baking.

CHEESE QUESADILLAS

SERVES 2 TO 4
PREP TIME: 5 MINUTES
COOK TIME: 10 MINUTES

PREPARE INGREDIENTS

2 (8-inch) flour tortillas
2/3 cup shredded Monterey Jack cheese
4 teaspoons vegetable oil

GATHER COOKING EQUIPMENT

Cutting board
Pastry brush
10-inch nonstick skillet
Tongs
Chef's knife

"Crispy. I like the add-ons."
—Clementine, 12

"Ham and cheese is the perfect combination."
—Lola, 9

START COOKING! ←—≪≪≪

1. Lay tortillas on cutting board. Sprinkle half of cheese over half of first tortilla. Fold tortilla in half, forming half-moon shape with cheese inside, and press to flatten. Repeat with second tortilla and remaining cheese.

2. Use pastry brush to brush top of each quesadilla with 1 teaspoon oil. Place quesadillas in 10-inch nonstick skillet, oiled sides down (see photo, right). Brush second side of each quesadilla with another 1 teaspoon oil.

3. Heat skillet over medium heat and cook until bottoms of quesadillas are crisp and well browned, 2 to 3 minutes.

4. Use tongs to flip quesadillas and cook until second sides are crisp and browned, 1 to 2 minutes. Turn off heat.

5. Slide quesadillas out of skillet and onto cutting board. Let cool for 2 minutes. Cut each quesadilla in half. Serve warm.

GRILLED CHEESE, MEXICAN STYLE

Quesadillas might just be the perfect snack. You need just three ingredients—flour tortillas, cheese, and some vegetable oil—and the recipe comes together really quickly. To make this recipe extra simple, use shredded cheese. If you have a block of cheese in the fridge, just run it over the large holes of a box grater (see photo, page 14).

Letting the quesadillas cool before cutting and serving them is important; straight from the skillet, the cheese is molten and will ooze out.

If you want to make quesadillas for a crowd, transfer the first batch to a rimmed baking sheet and keep it warm in a 200-degree oven. Go ahead and use more tortillas, cheese, and oil to make a second batch. Let all four quesadillas cool, and then slice and enjoy.

You can serve quesadillas as is (they are so good), but you can get fancy by serving quesadillas with a spoonful of sour cream, plain Greek yogurt, Quick Tomato Salsa (page 58), or Guacamole (page 60).

TWO IN A PAN

Folding quesadillas before cooking means you can cook two at a time in one skillet. Just make sure to arrange folded edges in center of skillet, with curved parts following curves of skillet.

MAKE IT YOUR WAY

In addition to topping it with sour cream, salsa, or guacamole, you can customize your quesadilla by adding 2 tablespoons total of any of these add-ins in whatever combination you like: **chopped tomatoes, chopped ham, chopped scallions, drained black beans, chopped cilantro, minced pickled jalapeños, canned chopped green chiles,** or even leftover **cooked chicken.** Sprinkle 2 tablespoons of your favorite add-in ingredients over one half of each tortilla after you sprinkle cheese in step 1.

"It was pretty easy to make, it didn't take very long, and it was delicious." —Simon, 10

"Very fun because I got to try a kind of cooking that I don't do often. I also learned a lot, like how to open a can and how to use a colander." —Greta, 10

NACHOS

SERVES 4 TO 6
PREP TIME: 10 MINUTES
COOK TIME: 25 MINUTES

PREPARE INGREDIENTS

1 (15-ounce) can pinto beans
4 ounces tortilla chips
1 cup shredded Monterey Jack cheese
2 scallions, sliced thin
1 cup tomato salsa (jarred or homemade, see page 58)
Greek yogurt or sour cream

GATHER COOKING EQUIPMENT

Colander
Can opener
½-cup dry measuring cup
8-by-8-inch square baking dish
Oven mitts
Cooling rack
Spoon

START COOKING!

1. Adjust oven rack to middle position and heat oven to 400 degrees. Set colander in sink. Open can of pinto beans and pour into colander. Rinse beans with cold water and shake colander to drain well. Measure out ½ cup beans; refrigerate remaining beans for another use.

2. Spread half of chips in even layer in 8-by-8-inch square baking dish. Sprinkle chips evenly with half of cheese.

3. Sprinkle beans over cheese, then sprinkle half of scallions on top. Repeat with remaining chips, cheese, and scallions.

4. Place baking dish in oven and bake until cheese is melted, 7 to 10 minutes. Use oven mitts to remove nachos from oven (ask an adult for help). Place baking dish on cooling rack. Let cool for 2 minutes.

5. Spoon half of salsa over top of nachos. Serve with remaining salsa and yogurt.

INSTANT FIESTA!

These nachos are a cinch to make and can turn after-school snack time for a few kids into something of a fiesta. Or double the recipe and use a 13-by-9-inch baking dish, and you'll have enough nachos to really get the party started! If you like your nachos spicy, layer in some drained pickled jalapeño chiles along with the scallions. Monterey Jack cheese melts well and is the classic choice for nachos, but cheddar works too.

"It was extraordinarily good! Best lemonade I have ever tasted." —Benedict, 11

REAL LEMONADE

SERVES 6 (MAKES ABOUT 5 CUPS)
PREP TIME: 5 MINUTES
COOK TIME: 20 MINUTES

PREPARE INGREDIENTS

7 lemons
¾ cup sugar
3½ cups cold water
Ice

GATHER COOKING EQUIPMENT

Cutting board
Chef's knife
Pitcher
Large bowl
Potato masher
Citrus juicer
Liquid measuring cup
Rubber spatula
Fine-mesh strainer
Tall glasses

WHEN LIFE GIVES YOU LEMONS

Mashing sliced lemon with granulated sugar extracts oils contained in the peel and punches up the lemon flavor. Try to purchase large lemons that give to gentle pressure; hard lemons have thicker skin and yield less juice.

Cut 1 lemon in ha lengthwise throug both ends. Lay lemo halves, flat side dow on cutting board, the cut each half crosswi into thin semicircles

START COOKING! ← ⫸

1. Cut 1 lemon in half lengthwise through both ends. Lay lemon halves, flat side down, on cutting board, then cut each half crosswise into thin semicircles (see photo, left); discard ends. Put half of slices in large pitcher and set aside. Put remaining slices in large bowl and add sugar.

2. Use potato masher to mash sugar and lemon slices together until sugar is completely wet, about 1 minute. Set aside.

3. Cut remaining 6 lemons in half crosswise. Use citrus juicer to squeeze juice into liquid measuring cup. You should have a little over 1 cup. (Save any extra juice for another use.)

4. Pour lemon juice and water into bowl with lemon slices and sugar. Use rubber spatula to stir mixture until sugar is completely dissolved, about 1 minute.

5. Set fine-mesh strainer over pitcher. Carefully pour mixture through strainer. Use rubber spatula to press on lemons to get out as much juice as possible. Discard lemon slices in strainer.

6. To serve, place ice in tall glasses and pour lemonade over ice. (Lemonade can be refrigerated for up to 3 days.)

→ MAKE IT YOUR WAY ←

Want a lemonade stand that will really attract attention? Try one of these fancy flavors—adults will pay a lot of money for a glass of these refreshing quenchers. Or try one of these fun flavors for your next sleepover or birthday party.

STRAWBERRY LEMONADE

Add ½ cup sliced strawberries to pitcher with lemon slices in step 1. Mash 1 cup sliced strawberries along with sugar and lemon slices in step 2.

WATERMELON LEMONADE

Mash 2 cups chopped seedless watermelon along with sugar and lemon slices in step 2. Use 3 cups (instead of 3½ cups) of cold water in step 4.

RASPBERRY LEMONADE

Mash 1 cup fresh or frozen raspberries along with sugar and lemon slices in step 2.

LIMEADE

Slice 2 limes instead of lemon in step 1. Squeeze juice from 10 limes instead of 6 lemons in step 3.

SWEET ICED TEA

SERVES 6 (MAKES ABOUT 1 QUART)
PREP TIME: 10 MINUTES
COOK TIME: 1 HOUR

PREPARE INGREDIENTS

6 decaffeinated black tea bags
4 cups plus 2 tablespoons water, room
    temperature, measured separately
2 tablespoons sugar
1 lemon
Ice

GATHER COOKING EQUIPMENT

Pitcher
Liquid measuring cup
Oven mitts
Small spoon
Chef's knife
Cutting board
Large spoon
Tall glasses

> "It was easy. Not a lot of stirring involved.
> It was fun." —James, 11
>
> "The recipe was easy to make. The directions
> were easy to follow. I do not think the tea
> was sweet enough." —Kara, 10

START COOKING!

1. Place tea bags and 4 cups water in pitcher. Let sit on counter for 45 minutes.

2. Meanwhile, in liquid measuring cup, combine sugar and remaining 2 tablespoons water. Heat in microwave for 30 seconds. Use oven mitts to remove measuring cup from microwave. Use small spoon to stir mixture constantly until sugar dissolves completely, about 30 seconds; set aside.

3. Cut lemon in half lengthwise through both ends. Place one half of lemon flat on cutting board and slice crosswise into thin half circles (see photo, page 68); discard ends. (Refrigerate other lemon half for another use.)

4. Remove tea bags from water and discard. Pour sugar mixture into tea and add lemon slices. Use large spoon to stir tea to combine. To serve, place ice in tall glasses and pour tea over ice. (Tea can be refrigerated for up to 3 days.)

MAKE IT YOUR WAY

Traditional sweet iced tea is made by adding sugar and lemon to black tea, but if you like green tea, try it instead. To add some zing to your tea, try these juicy combinations!

CRANBERRY-ORANGE ICED TEA

Use 1 cup cranberry juice and 3 cups water in step 1. Use ½ orange instead of ½ lemon in step 3.

POMEGRANATE-LIME ICED TEA

Use 1 cup pomegranate juice and 3 cups water in step 1. Use 1 whole lime instead of ½ lemon in step 3.

TEA, NO KETTLE

Steeping (a fancy word for soaking) tea bags in room-temperature water makes an especially mellow tea without any bitter notes, and you don't need to boil water in a kettle. Because the tea is never heated, use a sugar syrup (sugar dissolved in a little hot water) rather than trying to stir in granulated sugar (which won't dissolve in room temperature tea). This recipe uses the microwave to make the simple syrup. So easy.

BEST HOT CHOCOLATE

MAKES 12 CHOCOLATE BALLS, ENOUGH FOR
   TWELVE 1-CUP SERVINGS
PREP TIME: 5 MINUTES
COOK TIME: 20 MINUTES, PLUS 3 HOURS
   CHILLING TIME

PREPARE INGREDIENTS

2 cups semisweet chocolate chips
1 cup heavy cream
¼ teaspoon salt
Milk
Mini marshmallows (optional)
Whipped cream (optional)

GATHER COOKING EQUIPMENT

Large microwave-safe bowl
Oven mitts
Whisk
Plastic wrap
1-tablespoon measuring spoon
Large mugs
Liquid measuring cup
Small spoon

MAKE IT YOUR WAY

You can replace some of the chocolate chips with peanut butter baking chips (sometimes called "morsels") to make creamy, dreamy, peanutty hot chocolate balls.

PEANUTTY HOT CHOCOLATE

Use 1 cup peanut butter baking chips and 1 cup semisweet chocolate chips in step 1.

"Just like drinking fudge that was hot and melted."
—Benjamin, 10

START COOKING!

"It was delicious but it took a lot of patience waiting three long hours for the chocolate to set!" —Libby, 9

1. In large microwave-safe bowl, combine chocolate chips, cream, and salt. Heat in microwave for 30 seconds. Use oven mitts to remove bowl from microwave, then use whisk to stir mixture. Repeat microwaving and whisking every 30 seconds until chocolate is completely melted and mixture is smooth, about 1½ minutes.

2. Transfer bowl to refrigerator and let chill until firm, about 3 hours or overnight.

3. Lay small piece of plastic wrap on counter. Scoop 2 tablespoons of chocolate mixture onto plastic wrap and twist to form ball (see photos, below). Repeat with remaining chocolate mixture to form 12 balls. (Chocolate balls can be frozen for up to 2 months. When ready to use, proceed with step 4—no thawing needed.)

4. To make one serving of hot chocolate, place 1 chocolate ball in large mug. Pour ¾ cup milk over top. Heat in microwave for 30 seconds. Use oven mitts to remove mug from microwave, then use small spoon to stir mixture. Repeat heating and stirring every 30 seconds until chocolate ball is completely melted and mixture is hot, about 2 minutes.

5. Top with mini marshmallows and whipped cream (if using) and serve.

NO MORE PACKETS

Paper packets of hot cocoa mix are very convenient, but they don't taste all that great. You can make something way better yourself—hot chocolate balls—and then store the balls in the freezer so they're ready whenever you want a mug of hot chocolate.

1. Lay small piece of plastic wrap on counter. Use measuring spoon to scoop 2 tablespoons of chocolate mixture into center of plastic wrap.

2. Gather and pull edges of plastic wrap up around chocolate mixture and twist plastic wrap to form ball and seal tightly.

CHAPTER 3: COOKING FOR YOU

SANDWICHES, SOUPS, AND OTHER QUICK FIXES FOR LUNCH OR DINNER ON YOUR OWN (OR MAYBE WITH A LITTLE BROTHER OR SISTER).

CLASSIC GRILLED CHEESE SANDWICH

SERVES 1
PREP TIME: 5 MINUTES
COOK TIME: 10 MINUTES

PREPARE INGREDIENTS

2 slices hearty white or wheat
 sandwich bread
1 tablespoon unsalted butter,
 melted (see page 12 for
 how to melt butter)
½ cup shredded cheddar or
 Monterey Jack cheese

GATHER COOKING EQUIPMENT

Cutting board
Pastry brush
10-inch nonstick skillet
Spatula
Butter knife

"Delicious! Crispy and cheesy."
—Kellen, 12

"More buttery than Mom's
version."—Calla, 11

START COOKING!

1. Place bread slices on cutting board. Use pastry brush to brush melted butter evenly over 1 side of each slice.

2. Flip 1 slice over (buttered side down), sprinkle with cheese, and press down on cheese lightly. Place second slice of bread on top (butter on the outside) and press down gently.

3. Place sandwich in 10-inch nonstick skillet and press it lightly with spatula. Heat skillet over medium-low heat and cook until first side is golden brown, 3 to 5 minutes.

4. Use spatula to flip sandwich over and press lightly again. Cook until second side is golden brown and cheese is melted, about 2 minutes.

5. Turn off heat. Use spatula to transfer sandwich back to cutting board. Let cool for 2 minutes. Cut sandwich in half and serve warm.

THE WORLD'S EASIEST (AND BEST) SANDWICH

You need just three ingredients—bread, butter, and cheese—to make a proper grilled cheese sandwich. Start with shredded cheese (or do it yourself, running a block of cheese over the large holes of a box grater—see photo, page 14). Buttering the bread—not the pan—helps the sandwich brown evenly. Cooking the sandwich over medium-low heat allows the cheese to melt evenly, and pressing it lightly ensures that the bread has good contact with the pan and browns well. You can double the recipe and cook two sandwiches at a time in a 12-inch nonstick skillet.

 ## FLIPPING SANDWICHES WITH EASE

Flipping a sandwich in a hot pan can seem scary. But it's actually quite easy if you use the right tool and method. Ask an adult to help as you learn this technique. Flip burgers this way, too.

1. Slide spatula completely underneath sandwich. Make sure to use spatula large enough to hold sandwich.

2. Carefully place fingertips on top of sandwich. Lift spatula and flip sandwich over, moving your fingers out of the way as you flip sandwich onto second side.

"I was surprised at the taste. It was very good. I didn't think I'd like it, but I ended up loving it."
—Zoe, 11

"It was excellent and very delicious. The tomatoes made it a little sweet and yummy."
—Winston, 10

CAPRESE PANINI

SERVES 1
PREP TIME: 10 MINUTES
COOK TIME: 15 MINUTES

PREPARE INGREDIENTS

2 (½-inch-thick) slices crusty bread
1 tablespoon extra-virgin olive oil
½ cup shredded mozzarella cheese
1 small tomato, sliced into circles
Pinch salt
4 fresh basil leaves

GATHER COOKING EQUIPMENT

Cutting board
Pastry brush
10-inch nonstick skillet
Small, flat saucepan lid (smaller than skillet)
Oven mitts
Spatula
Chef's knife

PANINI IS ITALIAN FOR GRILLED CHEESE

In Italy, the combination of tomato, mozzarella, and basil is known as "Caprese," a reference to the island of Capri, where these ingredients are typically served together in a salad. These flavors translate perfectly to a crispy, toasty panini (a pressed Italian grilled cheese sandwich). Crusty slices of rustic bread are traditional in a panini, but hearty sandwich bread will work as well.

START COOKING!

1. Place bread slices on cutting board. Use pastry brush to brush oil evenly over 1 side of each slice.

2. Flip 1 slice over (oiled side down) and sprinkle with half of cheese. Place tomato slices on top and sprinkle with salt. Top with basil and remaining cheese. Place second slice of bread on top (oil on the outside).

3. Place sandwich in 10-inch nonstick skillet. Place saucepan lid on sandwich and press down firmly, then leave lid in place.

4. Heat skillet over medium heat and cook until bread is golden brown on bottom, about 4 minutes.

5. Use oven mitts to remove lid. Use spatula to flip sandwich over. Place lid back on sandwich and press down again. Cook until second side is golden brown and cheese is melted, about 2 minutes.

6. Turn off heat. Use spatula to transfer sandwich back to cutting board. Let cool for 2 minutes. Cut sandwich in half and serve warm.

WEIGH DOWN FOR CRISPNESS

A fancy panini press gets the bread really crisp. But don't worry: you can get the same results with any flat saucepan lid that's slightly smaller than your skillet. If you have a nonstick grill pan, use it in place of the nonstick skillet—the pan will put attractive grill marks on the panini.

Place saucepan lid on sandwich and press down firmly, then leave lid in place to weight sandwich while it cooks.

VEGGIE WRAP WITH HUMMUS

SERVES 1
PREP TIME: 10 MINUTES
COOK TIME: 15 MINUTES

PREPARE INGREDIENTS

2 teaspoons extra-virgin olive oil
1 teaspoon lemon juice, squeezed
    from ½ lemon
Pinch salt
Pinch pepper
1 carrot
1 avocado
1 (11-by-8-inch) piece lavash bread
⅓ cup plain hummus (store-bought
    or homemade, see page 54)
8 cherry tomatoes, cut in half
½ cup baby spinach

GATHER COOKING EQUIPMENT

Small bowl
Whisk
Vegetable peeler
Chef's knife
Cutting board
Box grater
Butter knife
Soupspoon

"Fun but messy." —Alison, 10

"Yummy." —Eliza, 11   "It was easy." —Katie, 9

→ VEGGIES RULE ←

Hummus and a mix of fresh veggies make a great wrap. For the bread, swap out the usual tortilla for lavash, a soft, thin Middle Eastern flatbread. (Of course, you can use a 10-inch flour tortilla if you like.) Spread a hefty amount of creamy hummus on your wrap, then add shredded carrots (tossed with a lemony dressing), juicy tomatoes, buttery sliced avocados, and baby spinach. You can double the ingredients in this recipe to make two wraps.

1. In small bowl, whisk oil, lemon juice, salt, and pepper together.

2. Use vegetable peeler to peel carrot. With knife, trim ends of carrot and discard. Holding thicker end, carefully run carrot over large holes of box grater to shred (stop when your fingers get close to grater and discard carrot end). Add shredded carrot to bowl with lemon dressing and stir to coat.

3. Use butter knife to cut avocado in half lengthwise around pit (see photos, page 37). With your hands, twist both halves in opposite directions to separate. Use soupspoon to remove pit. Use soupspoon to scoop 1 avocado half from skin onto cutting board; discard pit and skin (save remaining half for another use). Place avocado half flat side down on cutting board and chop.

4. Place lavash on clean counter. Use back of soupspoon to spread hummus over lavash, leaving ½-inch border around edge. Top with carrot mixture, avocado, tomatoes, and spinach.

5. Fold up bottom of lavash over filling. Fold in sides of lavash over filling, then roll tightly into log (see photos, right). Cut wrap in half. Serve.

HOW TO ROLL UP A WRAP

Whether using lavash or a tortilla, the technique for making a wrap sandwich is the same.

1. Fold up bottom of lavash or tortilla over filling. Then fold in sides of lavash or tortilla over filling.

2. Working from bottom up, roll into log, ending with seam side down. Don't roll too tightly or you will push filling out of open end as you roll.

SPICY BLT WRAP

SERVES 1
PREP TIME: 10 MINUTES
COOK TIME: 15 MINUTES

PREPARE INGREDIENTS

2 slices bacon
1 tablespoon mayonnaise
¼ teaspoon sriracha sauce
3 romaine lettuce leaves
6 cherry tomatoes, cut in half
1 (10-inch) flour tortilla

GATHER COOKING EQUIPMENT

Microwave-safe plate
Paper towels
Oven mitts
Medium bowl
Small spoon
Cutting board
Chef's knife

"At first I thought this would be kind of spicy when I saw the sriracha, but it isn't very spicy at all! Perfect for people who don't like spice very much. I would definitely make this again." —Chloe, 10

"My favorite part was the bacon!" —Ty, 8

1. Line microwave-safe plate with 2 paper towels and place bacon on top. Top with 2 more paper towels. Cook in microwave until crispy, 3 to 5 minutes. Use oven mitts to remove plate from microwave. Let bacon cool for 3 minutes.

2. In medium bowl, stir mayonnaise and sriracha with small spoon until combined.

3. Stack lettuce leaves on cutting board; trim ends and discard. Chop lettuce into 1-inch pieces.

4. Add lettuce and tomatoes to bowl with mayonnaise mixture. Use spoon to stir vegetables until well coated with dressing.

5. Place tortilla on clean counter. Place lettuce and tomatoes in center of tortilla, leaving 2-inch border around edge. Break bacon slices in half and place on top of lettuce and tomatoes. Fold up bottom of tortilla over filling. Fold in sides of tortilla over filling, then roll tightly into log (see photos, page 81). Cut wrap in half. Serve.

A BETTER BLT

The classic bacon, lettuce, and tomato sandwich is much easier to eat as a wrap sandwich. No layers sliding every which way, and no tomatoes or bacon falling onto your shirt. Cooking the bacon in the microwave is an easy hands-off method. The cooking time will vary depending on your microwave. If you like things extra spicy, use ½ teaspoon sriracha in step 2. This recipe can be doubled to make two wraps.

Place strips of raw bacon between layers of paper towels before they go into the microwave. Towels absorb grease and keep the bacon from making a mess inside your microwave.

HOT SAUCES OF THE WORLD

From Tabasco (bottled in Louisiana) to sriracha (originally from Thailand), hot sauces are made around the globe in warm places where chiles are grown. Sriracha is thicker than most other hot sauces and is not as spicy. It's also made with a little sugar, which balances the heat and explains why this particular hot sauce has become so popular. It's even on the menu at McDonald's. Mixed with a little mayonnaise, sriracha becomes a great sandwich spread or dipping sauce for chicken fingers.

PESTO FLATBREAD "PIZZA"

SERVES 1 TO 2
PREP TIME: 10 MINUTES
COOK TIME: 30 MINUTES

PREPARE INGREDIENTS

1 teaspoon extra-virgin olive oil
1 (8-inch) naan bread
2 tablespoons pesto
⅓ cup shredded mozzarella cheese
12 cherry tomatoes, cut in half

GATHER COOKING EQUIPMENT

Pastry brush
Ruler
Rimmed baking sheet
Small spoon
Oven mitts
Cooling rack
Spatula
Cutting board
Chef's knife or pizza wheel

MAKE IT YOUR WAY

To personalize your pizza, sprinkle a handful of your favorite toppings—in whatever combination you like—over the mozzarella. Some topping ideas: **sliced bell peppers**, **pepperoni**, **sliced scallions**, **chopped olives**, or dollops of **goat cheese** or **ricotta cheese**.

START COOKING!

1. Adjust oven rack to lowest position and heat oven to 400 degrees. Use pastry brush to brush oil into 9-inch circle in center of rimmed baking sheet. Place naan on top of oil on baking sheet.

2. Use back of small spoon to spread pesto over naan, leaving ½-inch border around edge. Sprinkle cheese over pesto, then sprinkle tomatoes over cheese.

3. Place baking sheet in oven and bake until naan is golden brown around edges, 8 to 10 minutes.

4. Use oven mitts to remove baking sheet from oven (ask an adult for help). Place baking sheet on cooling rack and let cool for 5 minutes.

5. Use spatula to carefully transfer naan to cutting board (baking sheet will be hot). Use chef's knife or pizza wheel to cut naan into wedges. Serve.

PIZZA IN A FLASH

Naan is an Indian flatbread with a chewy texture and a puffed, slightly charred crust. Brushing the baking sheet with olive oil and then baking the naan on the lowest rack in a 400-degree oven gives it a crispy texture—just like pizza crust. This recipe can be doubled.

HAM AND CHEESE SLIDERS

SERVES 2
PREP TIME: 5 MINUTES
COOK TIME: 20 MINUTES

PREPARE INGREDIENTS

4 teaspoons yellow mustard
4 potato dinner rolls, sliced open
4 slices deli ham
8 dill pickle chips
2 slices deli cheddar cheese, cut in half

GATHER COOKING EQUIPMENT

Rimmed baking sheet
Parchment paper
Butter knife
Oven mitts
Cooling rack
Spatula
2 plates

"It was very easy, and it tasted
like a grilled cheese but fancier.
My 7-year-old sister doesn't like
mustard but still ate it!" —Vivien, 9

"Easy-peasy. Fun to make."
—Vickie, 9

QUICK AND EASY SLIDERS

Take your ham and cheese sandwich to the next
level by turning it into a slider. Fluffy potato dinner
rolls are just the right size for a few bites. Heating
these small sandwiches in the oven makes the rolls
nice and crisp and the cheese melty and gooey.
You can also make these sliders in a toaster oven
if you have one. To make a whole bunch of sliders
for a party, double or triple this recipe (to make
8 or 12 sliders) and heat them all on one rimmed
baking sheet in the oven.

START COOKING! ←‹‹‹‹‹

1. Adjust oven rack to middle position and heat oven to 400 degrees. Line rimmed baking sheet with parchment paper.

2. Use butter knife to spread mustard evenly over insides of rolls.

3. Layer 1 slice ham, 2 pickle chips, and ½ slice cheese into each roll and press down gently (you should have 4 sliders).

4. Place sliders on baking sheet. Place baking sheet in oven and bake until cheese has melted and rolls are crisp, about 5 minutes.

5. Use oven mitts to remove baking sheet from oven (ask an adult for help) and transfer to cooling rack. Use spatula to carefully transfer sliders to 2 plates (baking sheet will be hot). Serve.

OVEN MITTS

Oven mitts should fit snuggly like a glove. Chances are the mitts in your kitchen are too big since they are made to fit even the biggest adult hands. Luckily, you can buy mitts designed for you. We gave three kid-friendly mitts to a panel of six boys and girls, ages 8 to 11. We asked our kitchen testers to try on the gloves to assess fit; pick up eight room-temperature pots and pans to evaluate grip; and load, rotate, and remove cookie sheets from a 350-degree oven to get a read on heat protection.

While all the kids liked the extra grippiness the neoprene mitts provided, this pair was far too small for all but the tester with the smallest hands. Instead, our kid testers preferred the two cotton models. The top pick, the **Williams Sonoma Junior Chef Oven Mitt ($7.95 per mitt)**, hugged big and small hands perfectly. And their extra length helped keep forearms safe, too.

ROASTED TOMATO AND CORN TOSTADAS

SERVES 2 TO 4
PREP TIME: 15 MINUTES
COOK TIME: 35 MINUTES

PREPARE INGREDIENTS

2½ cups cherry tomatoes, cut in half
½ cup frozen corn
1 tablespoon plus 1 teaspoon
    vegetable oil, measured separately
½ teaspoon chili powder (optional)
¼ teaspoon salt
½ cup refried beans
4 (6-inch) corn tostadas
½ cup crumbled queso fresco or
    feta cheese
¼ cup fresh cilantro leaves

GATHER COOKING EQUIPMENT

Medium bowl
Rubber spatula
13-by-9-inch baking dish
Small bowl
Small spoon
Rimmed baking sheet
Oven mitts
Cooling rack
Large spoon
Spatula
Plates

START COOKING!

1. Adjust oven rack to lower-middle position and heat oven to 400 degrees.

2. In medium bowl, use rubber spatula to stir tomatoes, corn, 1 tablespoon oil, chili powder (if using), and salt until well combined.

3. Spread tomato mixture into 13-by-9-inch baking dish. Place dish in oven and bake until tomatoes are soft, 20 to 25 minutes.

4. Meanwhile, in small bowl, stir refried beans and remaining 1 teaspoon oil until smooth. Use back of small spoon to spread beans evenly over tostadas. Place tostadas on rimmed baking sheet.

5. Use oven mitts to remove baking dish from oven (ask an adult for help) and transfer to cooling rack.

6. Use large spoon to spoon tomato mixture (be careful, baking dish will be hot) evenly over tostadas. Place baking sheet in oven and bake tostadas until beans are warm, about 5 minutes.

7. Use oven mitts to remove baking sheet from oven (ask an adult for help) and transfer to cooling rack. Sprinkle with cheese and cilantro. Use spatula to carefully transfer tostadas to plates (baking sheet will be hot). Serve.

TOSTADAS = SUPERSIZE TORTILLA CHIPS

Tostadas are crispy, flat corn tortillas sold in the supermarket. They are a great base for lots of quick meals and snacks. In this recipe they are topped with a flavorful combination of roasted tomatoes and corn plus refried beans. A sprinkling of queso fresco (a crumbly, mild Mexican cheese) adds creaminess and a slight tang, and cilantro brings freshness.

CRISPY VEGGIE BURGERS

SERVES 2
PREP TIME: 10 MINUTES
COOK TIME: 20 MINUTES

PREPARE INGREDIENTS

1 (15-ounce) can chickpeas
1 large egg
2 tablespoons plain Greek
   yogurt, plus extra for serving
2 teaspoons plus 2 teaspoons
   extra-virgin olive oil,
   measured separately
½ teaspoon curry powder
⅛ teaspoon salt
Pinch pepper
⅓ cup panko bread crumbs
3 scallions, sliced thin
2 leaves lettuce
2 hamburger buns

"It reminded me of a potato latke
but more filling." —Sarah, 12

"I liked the consistency and the subtle curry
flavor. The crispiness was great!" —Alex, 13

GATHER COOKING EQUIPMENT

Colander
Can opener
¾-cup dry measuring cup
Medium bowl
Whisk
Food processor

Rubber spatula
Ruler
10-inch nonstick skillet
Spatula

1. Set colander in sink. Open can of chickpeas and pour into colander. Rinse chickpeas with cold water and shake colander to drain well. Measure out ¾ cup chickpeas; reserve remaining chickpeas for another use.

2. In medium bowl, whisk egg, yogurt, 2 teaspoons oil, curry powder, salt, and pepper until well combined.

3. Place ¾ cup chickpeas, panko, and scallions in food processor. Lock lid in place. Hold down pulse button for 1 second, then release. Repeat until ingredients are roughly chopped with some large pieces remaining, 5 to 8 pulses.

4. Remove lid and carefully remove food processor blade (ask an adult for help). Transfer chickpea mixture to bowl with egg mixture. Use rubber spatula to gently stir ingredients until just combined.

5. Use your hands to divide chickpea mixture into 2 lightly packed balls. Gently flatten each ball into circle that measures 4 inches across.

6. Add remaining 2 teaspoons oil to 10-inch nonstick skillet and swirl skillet to coat evenly with oil. Place patties in skillet and cook over medium heat until well browned on first side, 4 to 6 minutes. Use spatula to gently flip patties (ask an adult for help). Cook until well browned on second side, 4 to 5 minutes. Turn off heat.

7. Put 1 lettuce leaf inside each bun. Use spatula to slide burgers into buns. Serve with more yogurt (for dipping or spreading inside buns) if you like.

HOMEMADE VEGGIE BURGERS

Buttery, nutty chickpeas make a great foundation for a satisfying veggie burger. A touch of curry powder adds a hint of warm spice. Panko are crispy Japanese-style bread crumbs—they help hold the patties together. Process the chickpea mixture just until there are some finely chopped chickpeas (to help the patties hold together) and some larger pieces (for a satisfying texture). Do not overprocess the mixture in step 3, or the burgers will have a mushy texture. To keep the patties from falling apart, wait until they are well browned on the first side before attempting to flip them.

"Crunchy and tangy." —Ella, 10

"It's delicious." —Benedict, 11

"I wish there were more carrots." —Allison, 10

BABY SPINACH SALAD WITH VEGGIES

SERVES 2
PREP TIME: 10 MINUTES
COOK TIME: 15 MINUTES

PREPARE INGREDIENTS

3 cups baby spinach
12 cherry tomatoes, cut in half
1 small carrot
1 small cucumber
3 tablespoons extra-virgin olive oil
1 tablespoon red wine vinegar
½ teaspoon Dijon mustard or mayonnaise
⅛ teaspoon salt
Pinch pepper

GATHER COOKING EQUIPMENT

Medium bowl
Vegetable peeler
Cutting board
Chef's knife
Small jar with lid
1-tablespoon measuring spoon
Tongs

SHAKE THINGS UP

For a simple vinaigrette, you can skip the tricky step of slowly whisking in oil to make an emulsion (a smooth mixture of liquids that normally do not mix—such as vinegar and oil). Just shake all the ingredients together in a lidded jar. A touch of Dijon mustard or mayonnaise (whichever you prefer) provides emulsifying power to keep the dressing smooth and balanced.

1. Place spinach and tomatoes in medium bowl.

2. Peel carrot, then trim ends. Use vegetable peeler to slice carrot into ribbons (see photo, right). Transfer carrot ribbons to bowl with other vegetables.

3. Peel cucumber, then slice in half lengthwise. Cut each half into thin half circles (see photo, right). Transfer to bowl with other vegetables.

4. In small jar, combine oil, vinegar, mustard, salt, and pepper. Cover jar tightly with lid and shake until mixture is well combined, about 30 seconds. Spoon 2 tablespoons dressing over salad. Use tongs to toss vegetables until well coated with dressing. Serve. (Leftover vinaigrette can be refrigerated for up to 3 days. Shake well before using.)

MAKE IT YOUR WAY

You can substitute 3 cups of your favorite baby greens or salad mix for the baby spinach. Sprinkle a few tablespoons of any of these ingredients over your salad to make it into a more complete meal: **cubed/crumbled cheese, toasted nuts, chopped avocado, shredded/chopped chicken, sliced hard-cooked egg,** or **rinsed chickpeas.**

VEGGIE MAGIC

MAKING CARROT RIBBONS

Use vegetable peeler to peel off 3 ribbons from 1 side of carrot (peeling away from you). Turn carrot and peel off 3 more ribbons. Continue to turn and peel ribbons from remaining carrot.

SLICING A CUCUMBER

Peel cucumber, then slice in half lengthwise (the long way). Place pieces flat side down on cutting board, then cut each piece into thin half-circle slices.

CREAMY DREAMY TOMATO SOUP

SERVES 1 TO 2 (MAKES 2 CUPS)
PREP TIME: 15 MINUTES
COOK TIME: 20 MINUTES

PREPARE INGREDIENTS

2 tablespoons extra-virgin olive oil
2 tablespoons chopped shallot
   (see page 13 for how to chop shallots)
1 garlic clove, peeled and minced
   (see page 13 for how to mince garlic)
1 (14.5-ounce) can diced tomatoes,
   opened
½ cup chicken or vegetable broth
1 slice hearty white sandwich bread,
   torn into 1-inch pieces
1 teaspoon packed brown sugar

GATHER COOKING EQUIPMENT

Large saucepan
Wooden spoon
Ladle
Blender
Dish towel
1 or 2 bowls or mugs

"It's really good. It's smooth. It tastes a lot more tomatoey than my mom's version." —Anton, 8

"I loved it! It was easy to make. My favorite thing was that it had a lot of tomato flavor and it was creamy." —Zoe, 9

MAKE IT YOUR WAY

A bowl of soup is like a blank piece of paper ready for your creative touches. Garnish bowls of Creamy Dreamy Tomato Soup and Gingery Carrot Soup (page 96) with any of the following: a handful of **croutons** (page 97), sprinkling of **minced fresh herbs** (chives and parsley are especially good), dollop of **yogurt** or **sour cream**, drizzle of **extra-virgin olive oil**, or **chopped nuts** or **sunflower seeds**.

START COOKING! ←—≪≪

1. In large saucepan, heat oil over medium-low heat for 1 minute (oil should be hot but not smoking). Add shallot and garlic and cook, stirring occasionally with wooden spoon, until softened and lightly browned, about 3 minutes.

2. Carefully pour tomatoes and their juice into saucepan.

3. Stir in broth, bread, and sugar. Increase heat to medium-high and bring to boil. Reduce heat to medium and cook, stirring occasionally, until bread starts to fall apart, about 5 minutes.

4. Turn off heat and slide saucepan to cool burner. Let tomato mixture cool for 5 minutes.

5. Use ladle to carefully transfer tomato mixture into blender jar (mixture will be hot; ask an adult for help). Place lid on top of blender and hold lid firmly in place with folded dish towel (see photo, right). Process until smooth, 1 to 2 minutes. Pour soup into bowls or mugs and serve.

↓↓↓↓ ↓↓↓↓↓
BLENDER SAFETY

When using the blender to puree soup or make a smoothie, follow two simple rules:

1. Don't fill the blender jar more than two-thirds full.

2. Make sure to hold the lid securely in place with a folded dish towel.

This second rule is especially important when pureeing hot soup—the steam in the blender can loosen the lid, and soup could shoot up in the air if you're not holding the lid in place. No one wants soup on the ceiling!

Once ingredients are in blender jar, place lid on top and hold it firmly in place with folded dish towel. Then turn on blender, keeping pressure on towel so lid stays in place.

GINGERY CARROT SOUP

SERVES 1 TO 2 (MAKES 2 CUPS)
PREP TIME: 10 MINUTES
COOK TIME: 30 MINUTES

PREPARE INGREDIENTS

1 tablespoon vegetable oil
8 ounces carrots, peeled and cut
    into 1-inch pieces
1 (1-inch) piece fresh ginger,
    peeled and chopped
    (see photos, right)
¼ teaspoon salt
1⅓ cups chicken or vegetable broth
⅓ cup milk

GATHER COOKING EQUIPMENT

Large saucepan with lid
Wooden spoon
Oven mitts
Ladle
Blender
Dish towel
1 or 2 bowls or mugs

GINGER PREP

1. Use side of small spoon to scrape skin from one end of large piece of ginger. Peel away skin from about 1 inch of ginger.

2. Use chef's knife to cut off peeled portion of ginger. Chop peeled ginger into small pieces.

"It doesn't taste spicy at all. It's very sweet." —Marta, 9

START COOKING!

"I liked the ginger. If you don't like spice, don't put in the ginger." —Ella, 10

1. In large saucepan, heat oil over medium heat for 1 minute (oil should be hot but not smoking). Add carrots, ginger, and salt and cook, stirring occasionally with wooden spoon, until lightly browned, about 5 minutes.

2. Stir in broth, increase heat to high, and bring to boil. Reduce heat to medium-low, cover, and simmer until carrots are very soft, about 15 minutes. Turn off heat and slide saucepan to cool burner. Use oven mitts to remove lid and let cool for 5 minutes.

3. Use ladle to carefully transfer carrots and liquid into blender jar (liquid will be hot; ask an adult for help). Add milk. Place lid on top of blender and hold lid firmly in place with folded dish towel (see photo, page 95). Process until smooth, about 1 minute. Pour soup into bowls or mugs and serve.

RECYCLE STALE BREAD FOR CROUTONS

Don't throw out stale bread. Seriously, don't. Baguettes, sliced sandwich bread, and even loaves of crusty white bread can be recycled into homemade croutons. Use a chef's knife to cut the bread into cubes (½-inch to ¾-inch cubes are ideal). Toss the cubes with olive oil and some salt, and then spread them out on a rimmed baking sheet. Bake them in a 350-degree oven, stirring once or twice so they brown evenly, until crisp and golden brown, about 15 minutes. Once cool, the croutons can be stored in an airtight container for a week or so. Use them in soups or salads.

BEST-EVER PASTA WITH BUTTER AND PARMESAN CHEESE

SERVES 1 TO 2
PREP TIME: 10 MINUTES
COOK TIME: 20 MINUTES

PREPARE INGREDIENTS

2 quarts water
4 ounces fettuccine
   or other long-strand pasta
1½ teaspoons salt
½ cup grated Parmesan cheese,
   plus extra for serving
1 tablespoon unsalted butter
Pinch pepper (optional)

GATHER COOKING EQUIPMENT

Large saucepan with lid
Tongs
Ladle
Liquid measuring cup
Colander
1-tablespoon measuring spoon
1 or 2 bowls

"I liked that I could do this by myself. It
turned out so good! It was really easy
but tasted yummy! Even my sister was
impressed I cooked it alone!" —Paul, 12

"My favorite part is when we used the ladle
to grab the water because it reminded me
of scooping fruit punch!" —Ross, 10

START COOKING!

1. In large saucepan, bring water to boil.

2. Carefully add pasta and salt to boiling water. Use tongs to bend pasta into water (ask an adult for help). Cook, stirring frequently, until pasta is al dente (tender but still a bit chewy), 10 to 12 minutes.

3. Turn off heat. Use ladle to carefully transfer ¼ cup cooking water to liquid measuring cup. Set colander in sink. Carefully drain pasta in colander (ask an adult for help). Return drained pasta to now-empty saucepan.

4. Add cheese, butter, and 2 table-spoons reserved cooking water to saucepan with pasta. Return saucepan to low heat.

5. Use tongs to toss and stir constantly to combine, about 30 seconds. Turn off heat, cover saucepan, and let pasta sit for 1 minute.

6. Toss and stir pasta constantly again until sauce thoroughly coats pasta and cheese is melted, about 30 seconds. (If sauce is too thick, thin as needed with remaining cooking water, 1 tablespoon at a time.)

7. Transfer pasta to bowl. Sprinkle with extra cheese and pepper (if using). Serve.

SIMPLE CAN BE AMAZING

Pasta with just butter and cheese might seem simple, but it actually has a fancy name when served in restaurants—fettuccine alfredo. To make this dish at home, use authentic Parmesan cheese from Italy (look for the Italian words "Parmigiano-Reggiano" on the rind of the cheese). Use a rasp grater or the small holes on a box grater to create very small, almost feathery shreds of cheese that will melt into a creamy sauce (see photo, page 14). When the cheese, butter pieces, and reserved pasta cooking water are stirred into the just-drained fettuccine, the dish will appear very watery. But don't fret: After a covered 1-minute rest and a vigorous stir, everything will come together in a creamy sauce.

MEASURING PORTIONS OF PASTA

If you don't have a kitchen scale, use this handy trick for measuring out dried strand pasta, such as fettuccine, spaghetti, or linguine: Grab a handful of dried noodles and bunch them together tightly in your fist. Place the ends of the pasta directly over one of the circles below; add or remove individual pieces until pasta just fills the circle.

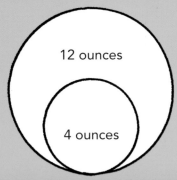

12 ounces

4 ounces

CHAPTER 4: COOKING FOR FAMILY & FRIENDS

MAKING DINNER IS A GREAT WAY TO UP YOUR COOKING GAME. AND NOTHING SAYS "I LOVE YOU" LIKE A HOME-COOKED MEAL.

"Tastes better than normal pasta. Less chunky in a good way." —Zoe, 13

ONE-POT PASTA WITH QUICK TOMATO SAUCE

SERVES 4
PREP TIME: 15 MINUTES
COOK TIME: 35 MINUTES

PREPARE INGREDIENTS

2 tablespoons extra-virgin olive oil,
  plus extra for drizzling
1 onion, peeled and chopped fine
  (see page 13 for how to chop onions)
1 teaspoon salt
4 garlic cloves, peeled and minced
  (see page 13 for how to mince garlic)
1 (28-ounce) can crushed tomatoes, opened
¼ teaspoon sugar
3¾ cups penne pasta
3 cups water
¼ cup chopped fresh basil (see page 13
  for how to chop herbs)
Grated Parmesan cheese

GATHER COOKING EQUIPMENT

Dutch oven
Wooden spoon
Ladle
Serving bowls

START COOKING!

1. In Dutch oven, heat oil over medium heat for 1 minute (oil should be hot but not smoking). Add onion and salt and cook, stirring often with wooden spoon, until onion is softened, about 5 minutes. Stir in garlic and cook for 30 seconds.

2. Stir in tomatoes and sugar. Reduce heat to medium-low and simmer gently, stirring occasionally, for 10 minutes.

3. Carefully stir in pasta and water. Increase heat to medium-high and cook, stirring often, until pasta is tender, 16 to 18 minutes.

4. Turn off heat. Drizzle pasta with extra oil and sprinkle basil over top. Use ladle to divide pasta and sauce among individual bowls. Serve with Parmesan cheese.

COOKING PASTA AND SAUCE TOGETHER

Rather than boiling the pasta in a pot of water, draining it, and then combining the cooked pasta with the sauce, you can actually cook dried pasta right in the sauce (which means no extra pot or colander to wash!). To help the pasta cook evenly, it's important to add a measured amount of water to the pot with the sauce. By the time the pasta is cooked, the sauce will be the perfect consistency and the pasta will have absorbed some of the sauce, so it will taste better. Talk about win/win.

SESAME NOODLES WITH SNOW PEAS AND CARROTS

SERVES 4 TO 6
PREP TIME: 20 MINUTES
COOK TIME: 25 MINUTES

PREPARE INGREDIENTS

½ cup creamy peanut butter
3 tablespoons lime juice, squeezed from
    2 limes, plus lime wedges
3 tablespoons soy sauce
2 tablespoons tahini
1 tablespoon honey
2 garlic cloves, peeled and minced
    (see page 13 for how to mince garlic)
½ teaspoon ground ginger
¼ cup hot water
1 carrot
1 pound fresh Chinese noodles or
    12 ounces dried linguine (see page 99
    for how to measure dried pasta)
6 ounces snow peas, strings removed
    (see photo, right) and cut in half

GATHER COOKING EQUIPMENT

Dutch oven   Cutting board
Large bowl   Box grater
Whisk   Tongs
Vegetable peeler   Colander
Chef's knife   Oven mitts

SNOW PEA PREP

Snap off tip of snow pea and grasp string. Pull string along flat side of snow pea to remove it. Cut peas in half crosswise.

START COOKING!

1. In Dutch oven or large pot, bring 4 quarts water to boil over high heat.

2. Meanwhile, in large bowl, whisk peanut butter, lime juice, soy sauce, tahini, honey, garlic, and ginger until smooth. Whisk in hot water until fully incorporated into sauce.

3. Use vegetable peeler to peel carrot. Use chef's knife to trim ends of carrot. Discard trimmed ends. Holding thicker end of carrot, carefully run carrot over large holes of box grater to shred (stop when your fingers get close to grater and discard carrot end).

4. Add noodles to boiling water in Dutch oven (ask an adult for help). Cook, stirring often with tongs, until noodles are tender, about 3 minutes if using fresh noodles or 10 to 12 minutes if using dried.

5. Ask an adult to pour noodles and water into colander (use oven mitts to hold hot pot). Rinse noodles under cold running water. Drain noodles well.

6. Transfer noodles to bowl with sauce. Add carrot and snow peas. Use tongs to combine noodles, vegetables, and sauce. Serve with lime wedges.

"I really liked the flavor. I didn't think the peanut butter would be good but it was!"
—Alex, 12

"Very peanut buttery. Lots of noodles."
—Tessa, 9

PERFECT PEELER

A peeler is a must when preparing carrots, potatoes, and apples. We tested five models: three geared for kids, our favorite peeler for adults, and a "palm peeler" that slides onto your middle finger like a ring. After preliminary testing by adults in our test kitchen, we eliminated two models: the peeler with a plastic blade rather than the usual metal blade (it was ineffective) and the palm peeler (it seemed unsafe).

We then recruited kids, ages 9 to 12, to test the top three models. Like adults, the kids preferred the sharpest blades because they made peeling easy, even when working with bumpy potatoes and slippery apples. The straight peeler wasn't as sharp as the two models with Y-shaped handles. Also, both Y-shaped peelers have more comfortable handles.

Between the top models, preferences came down to age and cooking experience. Older children gave the highest scores to our favorite peeler for adults, the **Kuhn Rikon Original Swiss Peeler ($5)**. Younger testers preferred **Le Petit Chef Peeler by Opinel ($17)**, thanks to the ring that sits between the blade and handle, where you can rest your index finger. As one kid tester said, it provided "a better grip, which meant more control."

Kuhn Rikon Original Swiss Peeler

Le Petit Chef Peeler by Opinel

PESTO TURKEY MEATBALLS WITH MARINARA SAUCE

SERVES 4
PREP TIME: 10 MINUTES
COOK TIME: 45 MINUTES

PREPARE INGREDIENTS

Vegetable oil spray
1 pound 93 percent lean ground
   turkey
¾ cup pesto
½ cup panko bread crumbs
¼ teaspoon salt
¼ teaspoon pepper
1 tablespoon extra-virgin olive oil
2 garlic cloves, peeled and minced
   (see page 13 for how to mince
   garlic)
1 (28-ounce) can crushed tomatoes,
   opened

GATHER COOKING EQUIPMENT

Rimmed baking sheet
Aluminum foil
Large bowl
1-tablespoon measuring spoon
Dutch oven
Wooden spoon
Oven mitts
Cooling rack
Tongs
Instant-read thermometer

"Absolutely delicious! Even my little brother told me he was proud of me and he ate two helpings!"
—Beatrice, 9

1. Adjust oven rack to middle position and heat oven to 450 degrees. Line rimmed baking sheet with aluminum foil. Spray foil with vegetable oil spray.

2. In large bowl, combine turkey, pesto, panko, salt, and pepper. Use your hands to gently mix until well combined.

3. Lightly wet your hands. Use your wet hands to roll turkey mixture into 16 meatballs (see photo, right). Arrange meatballs evenly on baking sheet. Wash your hands.

4. Place baking sheet in oven and bake until meatballs are just beginning to brown, about 15 minutes.

5. While meatballs bake, add oil to Dutch oven. Heat over medium heat for 1 minute (oil should be hot but not smoking). Stir in garlic with wooden spoon and cook for 30 seconds. Stir in tomatoes and bring to boil. Reduce heat to medium-low and simmer, stirring occasionally, for 10 minutes.

6. Use oven mitts to remove baking sheet with meatballs from oven (ask an adult for help). Place baking sheet on cooling rack.

7. Use tongs to carefully transfer meatballs to sauce in Dutch oven. Cook, gently stirring occasionally, until meatballs are cooked through and register 165 degrees on instant-read thermometer, about 5 minutes. (See page 117 for how to use thermometer.) Turn off heat. Serve.

FORMING MEATBALLS

Measure out 2 tablespoons turkey mixture. Use wet hands (mixture will be sticky) to gently roll turkey mixture into ball. Place meatball on baking sheet lined with greased foil.

EASY MEATBALLS

For a new spin on meatballs, add basil pesto for big flavor. The pesto replaces the minced herbs, minced garlic, and grated cheese in standard meatball recipes. Buy pesto from the refrigerated section of the supermarket—it has a fresher flavor than the jarred pesto sold in the grocery aisles. Serve these meatballs and sauce with 12 ounces of cooked pasta or on toasted sub rolls.

PULLED BBQ CHICKEN SANDWICHES

SERVES 4
PREP TIME: 15 MINUTES
COOK TIME: 25 MINUTES

PREPARE INGREDIENTS

½ cup ketchup
1 tablespoon molasses
1 tablespoon Dijon mustard
1 tablespoon cider vinegar
1 tablespoon Worcestershire sauce
1 tablespoon vegetable oil
2 tablespoons finely chopped shallot (see page 13 for how to chop shallots)
¾ teaspoon chili powder
¼ teaspoon salt
2 (8-ounce) boneless, skinless chicken breasts, cut in half lengthwise (see photo, right)
4 hamburger buns

GATHER COOKING EQUIPMENT

Liquid measuring cup
Whisk
12-inch skillet with lid
Rubber spatula
Tongs
Oven mitts

Instant-read thermometer
Large plate
2 forks
Soupspoon

"I liked how easy it was to make. The hardest part was shredding the chicken." —David, 11

→ BBQ, NO GRILL ←

Start by making a sweet and tangy barbecue sauce in a skillet and then cook the chicken right in the sauce, which helps it absorb lots of great flavor. Two forks make quick work of shredding (or "pulling") the cooked chicken (it's even quicker if you ask a sibling or friend to help!). Add **pickle chips**, **coleslaw**, **lettuce**, and/or **sliced avocado** to dress up the sandwiches.

START COOKING! ←≪≪≪≪

1. In liquid measuring cup, whisk together ketchup, molasses, mustard, vinegar, and Worcestershire sauce. Set aside.

2. In 12-inch skillet, heat oil over medium heat for 1 minute (oil should be hot but not smoking). Add shallot, chili powder, and salt. Cook, stirring occasionally with rubber spatula, until shallot is softened, about 3 minutes. Stir in ketchup mixture, scraping up any browned bits.

3. Use tongs to carefully place chicken in skillet. Bring mixture to boil. Reduce heat to medium-low, cover, and simmer for 4 minutes.

4. Use oven mitts to remove lid. Use clean tongs to flip chicken pieces over. Cover and simmer until chicken registers 165 degrees on instant-read thermometer, 4 to 6 minutes. (See page 117 for how to use thermometer.) Turn off heat. Slide skillet to cool burner.

5. Use clean tongs to transfer chicken to large plate. Let cool slightly, then use 2 forks to shred chicken into bite-size pieces (see photo, below). Return shredded chicken to skillet and stir to coat with sauce.

6. Heat chicken over medium heat until warmed through, 1 to 2 minutes. Turn off heat. Use soupspoon to evenly divide shredded chicken between hamburger buns. Serve.

SLICING CHICKEN

Use chef's knife to cut chicken breast in half lengthwise (the long way).

SHREDDING CHICKEN

Use 2 forks to pull cooked chicken apart and shred into bite-size pieces.

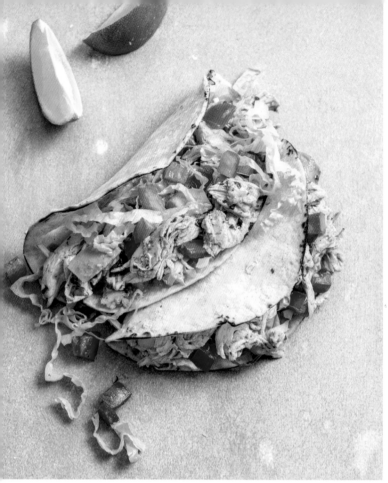

"Nicely coated with sauce. Easy but took a long time." —Clare, 11

SHREDDED CHICKEN TACOS

SERVES 4
PREP TIME: 15 MINUTES
COOK TIME: 30 MINUTES

PREPARE INGREDIENTS

2 tablespoons vegetable oil
4 garlic cloves, peeled and minced
  (see page 13 for how to mince
  garlic)
½ teaspoon chili powder
¼ teaspoon salt
½ cup orange juice
1 tablespoon Worcestershire sauce
2 (8-ounce) boneless, skinless chicken
  breasts, cut in half lengthwise (see
  photo, page 109)
¼ cup chopped fresh cilantro (see
  page 13 for how to chop herbs)
8 (6-inch) flour or corn tortillas

GATHER COOKING EQUIPMENT

12-inch skillet with lid
Wooden spoon
Tongs
Oven mitts
Instant-read thermometer
Large plate
2 forks
Microwave-safe plate
Dish towel

START COOKING!

1. In 12-inch skillet, heat oil over medium heat for 1 minute (oil should be hot but not smoking). Use wooden spoon to stir in garlic, chili powder, and salt and cook for 30 seconds. Stir in orange juice and Worcestershire sauce.

2. Use tongs to carefully place chicken in skillet. Bring mixture to boil. Reduce heat to medium-low, cover, and simmer for 4 minutes.

3. Use oven mitts to remove lid. Use clean tongs to flip chicken pieces over. Cover and simmer until chicken registers 165 degrees on instant-read thermometer, 4 to 6 minutes. (See page 117 for how to use thermometer.) Use clean tongs to transfer chicken to large plate.

4. Cook liquid left in skillet until thickened, 3 to 5 minutes. Turn off heat and slide skillet to cool burner.

5. Use 2 forks to shred chicken into bite-size pieces (see photo, page 109). Return shredded chicken to skillet and stir to coat with sauce.

6. Heat chicken over medium heat until warmed through, 1 to 2 minutes. Turn off heat and stir in cilantro. Cover to keep warm.

7. Stack tortillas on microwave-safe plate and cover with damp dish towel. Heat in microwave until warm, about 1 minute. Serve chicken in warmed tortillas with your favorite toppings.

SHREDDING LETTUCE

Thinly sliced lettuce (also called shredded lettuce) adds crunch to tacos. Crisp romaine lettuce is the perfect choice, but iceberg works too.

Discard any wilted outer leaves. Holding lettuce firmly with one hand, cut crosswise (the short way) to make thin strips.

MAKE IT YOUR WAY

Tacos are so much fun because everyone can assemble them right at the table—a homemade taco bar! Serve each topping in its own little bowl. **Shredded romaine lettuce** and **chopped tomatoes** are classic choices, but try **baby spinach**, **shredded cheese**, **diced avocado** (see page 37 for how to pit an avocado), **sour cream**, **hot sauce**, and/or **lime wedges**.

CRISPY OVEN-FRIED CHICKEN

SERVES 4
PREP TIME: 10 MINUTES
COOK TIME: 1½ HOURS

PREPARE INGREDIENTS

2 cups buttermilk
2 tablespoons Dijon mustard
Salt and pepper
1 teaspoon garlic powder
3 pounds bone-in chicken pieces (split
    breasts, drumsticks, and/or thighs)
Vegetable oil spray
4 cups cornflakes
1 teaspoon poultry seasoning
1 teaspoon paprika

GATHER COOKING EQUIPMENT

2 large bowls
Whisk
Paper towels
Plastic wrap
Rimmed baking sheet
Aluminum foil
2 cooling racks
Large zipper-lock plastic bag
Rolling pin
Instant-read thermometer
Oven mitts

"Awesome. One of my favorite chicken recipes."
—Jonathon, 8

SECRETS TO TENDER, JUICY CHICKEN

Soaking the chicken in seasoned buttermilk guarantees that your crispy chicken will come out of the oven moist and juicy on the inside. Salt doesn't just enhance flavor—when you soak meat in a salty solution (a brine), the salt reshapes protein molecules and helps them hold onto moisture when the meat is cooked. Buttermilk contains lactic acid, which is a mild acid that gently breaks down some proteins and makes chicken more tender.

START COOKING! ←≪≪≪

1. In large bowl, whisk together buttermilk, mustard, 2 teaspoons salt, ½ teaspoon pepper, and garlic powder.

2. Use paper towel to grasp skin on one piece of chicken, then pull off and discard skin. Repeat with remaining pieces of chicken. Add chicken to buttermilk mixture and turn to coat well. Wash your hands. Cover bowl with plastic wrap and refrigerate for at least 30 minutes or overnight.

3. Adjust oven rack to middle position and heat oven to 400 degrees. Line rimmed baking sheet with aluminum foil and set cooling rack inside baking sheet. Spray rack with vegetable oil spray.

4. Place cornflakes in large zipper-lock bag. Add poultry seasoning and paprika. Seal bag and shake to combine. Use rolling pin to crush cornflakes into small pieces (see photos, right). Pour cornflake mixture into second large bowl.

5. Remove one piece of chicken from buttermilk mixture, add to bowl with cornflake mixture, and toss to coat. Use your hands to gently press crumbs onto all sides of chicken. Place chicken on greased rack in baking sheet. Repeat with remaining pieces of chicken. Wash your hands.

6. Spray chicken all over with vegetable oil spray until each piece is shiny. Place baking sheet in oven and bake until chicken breasts register 165 degrees on instant-read thermometer and drumsticks/thighs register 175 degrees, 35 to 45 minutes. (See page 117 for how to use thermometer.)

7. Use oven mitts to remove baking sheet from oven (ask an adult for help). Place baking sheet on second cooling rack and let cool for 5 minutes. Serve.

SKINNING CHICKEN

Use paper towel to grasp slippery skin. Pull off skin and discard. You can use kitchen shears to trim any stubborn bits of skin on drumsticks.

☾ CORNFLAKES FOR DINNER ◡

1. Press rolling pin back and forth over zipper-lock bag until cornflakes are broken into small pieces.

2. Turn chicken pieces in crumbs to coat. Use your hands to gently press crumbs onto chicken so they stick.

"I loved the chicken. It was juicy and crunchy. The cornflake topping was so yummy! I couldn't stop snacking on the cornflakes." —Tristan, 11

TURKEY BURGERS

SERVES 4
PREP TIME: 10 MINUTES
COOK TIME: 20 MINUTES

PREPARE INGREDIENTS

1 pound 93 percent lean ground turkey
1 cup panko bread crumbs
½ cup shredded Monterey Jack cheese
¼ cup mayonnaise
Salt and pepper
1 tablespoon vegetable oil
4 hamburger buns

GATHER COOKING EQUIPMENT

Large bowl
Ruler
Large plate
12-inch nonstick skillet
Spatula
Instant-read thermometer

"I liked using my hands to mix up the meat. It was really easy to make. It was really yummy."
—Marta, 9

"I really liked the crispness of it. I really liked how well it went with the sriracha-lime spread."
—Roan, 12

A BETTER BURGER

Turkey burgers can be delicious as long as they aren't too dry. Be sure to buy 93 percent lean ground turkey (99 percent fat-free ground turkey breast will be very dry). Also, mixing the cheese right into the burgers helps keep the meat moist. The panko bread crumbs (crispy Japanese-style bread crumbs) and a little bit of mayonnaise lighten up the burgers and hold the patties together.

START COOKING! ←≪≪

1. In large bowl, use your hands to gently mix together turkey, panko, cheese, mayonnaise, ¼ teaspoon salt, and ⅛ teaspoon pepper.

2. Use your hands to divide turkey mixture into 4 lightly packed balls. Gently flatten each ball into circle that measures 4 inches across. Place patties on large plate. Wash your hands.

3. In 12-inch nonstick skillet, heat oil over medium heat for 1 minute (oil should be hot but not smoking). Tilt and swirl skillet to coat evenly with oil.

4. Use spatula to carefully place patties in skillet. Cook, without moving patties, until well browned on first side, about 5 minutes. Use clean spatula to gently flip patties (ask an adult for help). Cook until burgers register 165 degrees on instant-read thermometer, about 5 minutes. (See page 117 for how to use thermometer.)

5. Turn off heat. Use clean spatula to transfer burgers to hamburger buns. Add your favorite burger toppings and serve.

  # BURGER TOPPINGS

Top these burgers with any of the usual favorites, including **lettuce**, **pickles**, or **sliced tomato**. Or spice things up by making a quick batch of this "special" sauce: in medium bowl, whisk together ½ cup mayonnaise, 1 tablespoon sriracha, and 1 tablespoon lime juice.

APPLE CIDER–GLAZED PORK CHOPS

SERVES 4
PREP TIME: 10 MINUTES
COOK TIME: 25 MINUTES

PREPARE INGREDIENTS

½ cup apple cider
2 tablespoons maple syrup
2 teaspoons Dijon mustard
1 teaspoon minced fresh thyme (see page 13 for how to mince herbs) or ¼ teaspoon dried
4 boneless pork chops, ¾ to 1 inch thick
½ teaspoon salt
⅛ teaspoon pepper
1 tablespoon vegetable oil

GATHER COOKING EQUIPMENT

Liquid measuring cup
Whisk
Kitchen shears
Paper towels
12-inch skillet
Tongs

Instant-read thermometer
Serving platter
Aluminum foil
Rubber spatula
Large spoon

"Super fun to make and also tastes good. It's like restaurant food!" —Gabriella, 11

"It looks fancy but it's something you can do yourself (with a little help)." —Zoe, 10

HOW TO PREP PORK CHOPS

To prevent pork chops from curling up as they cook, use kitchen shears to make 2 small slits through fat on edges of each pork chop, about 2 inches apart. Cut through fat only, not meat.

START COOKING! ←⫷⫷⫷⫷

1. In liquid measuring cup, whisk together apple cider, maple syrup, mustard, and thyme. Set aside.

2. Use kitchen shears to make 2 cuts through fat on edges of each pork chop (see photo, above). Pat chops dry with paper towels and sprinkle both sides evenly with salt and pepper. Wash your hands.

3. In 12-inch skillet, heat oil over medium heat for 1 minute (oil should be hot but not smoking). Tilt and swirl skillet to coat evenly with oil.

4. Use clean tongs to carefully place chops in skillet. Cook, without moving chops, until well browned on first side, about 5 minutes.

5. Use clean tongs to carefully flip chops. Reduce heat to medium-low. Carefully pour apple cider mixture into skillet. Cook until chops register 145 degrees on instant-read thermometer, about 5 minutes. (See below for how to use thermometer.) Use clean tongs to transfer chops to serving platter. Cover platter with aluminum foil.

6. Increase heat to medium and cook apple cider mixture in skillet, stirring often with rubber spatula, until thick and syrupy, 2 to 3 minutes (sauce will be very bubbly when it thickens). Turn off heat. Spoon glaze over chops and serve.

→⇢ IS IT DONE YET? ⇠←

There's only one reliable way to know when chicken, meat, or fish is cooked—an instant-read thermometer. To check the temperature, insert the tip of the thermometer into the center of the thickest part of the food, making sure to avoid any bones. And ask an adult for help; the food—and the pan—are likely very hot.

For smaller cuts, such as chicken breasts or pork chops, use tongs to lift each piece out of the pan and then insert the thermometer sideways into the center of the food.

BEEF AND BROCCOLI STIR-FRY

SERVES 4
PREP TIME: 15 MINUTES
COOK TIME: 35 MINUTES

PREPARE INGREDIENTS

1 tablespoon plus ¼ cup water,
    measured separately
2 tablespoons soy sauce
1½ teaspoons cornstarch
¼ teaspoon baking soda
1 pound flank steak
¼ cup hoisin sauce
2 teaspoons Asian chili-garlic sauce
1 tablespoon vegetable oil
6 cups broccoli florets, cut into 1-inch
    pieces
4 garlic cloves, peeled and minced (see
    page 13 for how to mince garlic)

GATHER COOKING EQUIPMENT

2 medium bowls
Whisk
Cutting board
Chef's knife
Ruler
Rubber spatula
12-inch nonstick skillet
Large plate

SOFT AS VELVET

Stir-fries cook very quickly, which doesn't allow much time for meat to get tender. To avoid chewy beef, this recipe calls for two special ingredients: baking soda and cornstarch. Baking soda keeps the meat tender, and cornstarch gives the beef a thin, sticky coating that protects it from the heat of the skillet. This is called "velveting," and it's a trick used in Chinese restaurants to keep meat soft and silky. Bonus: The cornstarch also helps make the sauce thick and glossy. Serve this stir-fry with rice (see page 148 for how to cook rice).

1. In medium bowl, whisk 1 tablespoon water, soy sauce, cornstarch, and baking soda until combined.

2. Use chef's knife to cut steak into ¼-inch-thick slices (see photos, below). Add sliced beef to bowl with soy sauce mixture. Wash your hands. Use rubber spatula to stir to coat. Let beef sit for 15 minutes.

3. While beef sits, in second medium bowl, whisk hoisin sauce, chili-garlic sauce, and remaining ¼ cup water until combined.

4. When beef is ready, heat oil in 12-inch nonstick skillet over medium-high heat for 1 minute (oil should be hot but not smoking). Use rubber spatula to carefully add beef to skillet and spread it into even layer. Cook, stirring occasionally, until beef is lightly browned on both sides, 2 to 4 minutes. Turn off heat and use clean rubber spatula to transfer beef to large plate.

5. Add hoisin mixture, broccoli, and garlic to skillet and return to medium high-heat. Cook, stirring occasionally, until sauce is thickened and broccoli is tender, about 5 minutes.

6. Stir beef and juices on plate back into skillet and cook for 1 minute. Turn off heat. Serve.

CUTTING BEEF FOR STIR FRY

1. Use chef's knife to cut steak with grain (long lines running length of steak) into 3 or 4 strips (each about 2 inches wide).

2. Cut each strip across grain into thin slices, about ¼ inch thick.

KNIVES 101

Ask restaurant chefs to name the most important equipment in their kitchen and you will get one answer: knives. For new cooks, knives can seem scary—yes, they are sharp! But knives help us do so much in the kitchen. Here's what you need to know.

TWO ESSENTIAL KNIVES

While chefs often come to work with a pouch that holds a dozen knives, at home you need just two.

Chef's Knife: You will use this knife for 9 out of 10 kitchen tasks, from mincing herbs and chopping vegetables to slicing meat. A chef's knife with an 8-inch blade is best for adults, but kids are much better off with something smaller (see recommendations, right).

Paring Knife: This small knife is for precision work, such as cutting out the core from a ripe tomato or the hull (the leafy green part) from a strawberry. A paring knife's blade is typically 3.5 inches long and a little bit flexible.

CHEF'S KNIFE

HEEL

TIP

HANDLE

BLADE

PARING KNIFE

THE ALL-IMPORTANT CHEF'S KNIFE

While you can use a regular paring knife, we recommend buying a chef's knife designed just for kids. To find the best options, we tested five chef's knives for kids as well as the 6-inch version of our favorite knife for adults. Here's what our 12 kid testers, ages 8 to 13, found.

Two knives with serrated blades were so dull that we pulled them out of the testing. They simply weren't safe for kids (or adults). Also, the model with a bulky plastic blade was more like a saw. Ultimately, a good knife for kids is just like a good knife for adults—only smaller.

So what did our kid testers like? Although preferences changed with age and hand size, all our testers liked the **Misono Child's Mini Knife ($59)**. This Japanese knife has a sharp, nimble blade as well as a round tip that helps prevent accidental nicks. The handle wasn't all that comfortable, which kept this knife from being a favorite, but it was the one knife that earned good marks from both younger and older kids.

The 8- and 9-year-olds gave top marks to the **Opinel Le Petit Chef Cutlery Set ($45)**. It has a comfortable wooden handle with a finger hole to encourage a safe grip. It also comes with a small, shield-shaped plastic finger guard that kids can use on the hand holding the food. The 4-inch blade was sharp enough to be effective, with a rounded nose that prevents accidental nicks.

The 12- and 13-year-olds preferred the smaller version of our favorite adult chef's knife. The **Victorinox Swiss Army Fibrox Pro 6-Inch Chef's Knife ($21)** is super sharp and nimble. The lightweight, grippy handle is comfy, and the blade cuts food quickly and easily. The pointed tip requires some extra caution.

Preferences for 10- and 11-year-old testers aligned with kitchen experience and hand size—testers in this group with little experience and/or small hands liked the Opinel knife, while testers with some experience and/or larger hands agreed with the older kids and preferred the Victorinox.

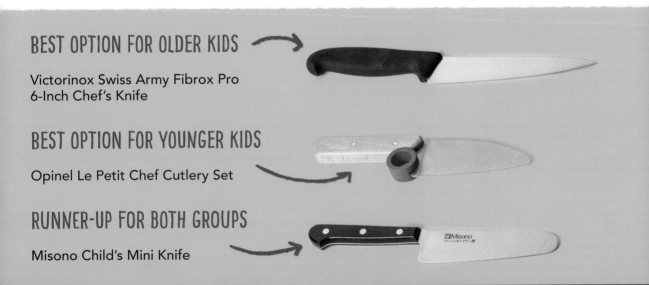

BEST OPTION FOR OLDER KIDS

Victorinox Swiss Army Fibrox Pro
6-Inch Chef's Knife

BEST OPTION FOR YOUNGER KIDS

Opinel Le Petit Chef Cutlery Set

RUNNER-UP FOR BOTH GROUPS

Misono Child's Mini Knife

HOW TO HOLD A CHEF'S KNIFE

A knife is only as good as the person using it. You must hold the knife correctly. And don't forget about your other hand—the one that holds the food securely in place while you cut. Practice these steps with an adult to become a knife wizard.

1. **Control Grip:** For more control, choke up on handle and actually grip blade between your thumb and forefinger. This grip works best for most kids.

2. **Force Grip:** For more power, wrap your hand around handle with your thumb tucked under curve of handle. This grip works best when cutting through hard foods such as carrots.

3. **Protect Your Fingertips:** Always use "bear claw" grip to hold food in place and minimize danger. Tuck your fingertips in, keeping them away from knife. During upward part of slicing motion, reposition your guiding hand for next cut.

→ SHARP KNIVES = SAFE KNIVES ←

A dull knife is an accident waiting to happen. That's because a dull knife is much more likely to slip off food. A dull knife is also a slow knife. Ask an adult to run the test below to determine if your chef's knife is sharp. If your knife is dull, ask an adult to sharpen it. We recommend electric and manual sharpeners made by Chef'sChoice.

Determining Sharpness: With one hand, hold single piece of printer paper firmly at top. Using your other hand, draw blade down through paper, heel to tip. If knife fails to slice paper cleanly, it's ready to be sharpened.

BASIC CUTTING MOTIONS

Depending on the food being prepared, you will use different parts of the knife blade and different motions. Here are three basic motions to practice.

SMALL ITEMS: KEEP TIP DOWN

To cut small items, such as celery or scallions, push blade forward and down, using blade's curve to guide middle of knife through food. Tip of blade should touch board at all times.

LARGE ITEMS: LIFT BLADE

To cut large items, such as eggplant, lift entire blade off board to help make smooth strokes through food.

MINCING: USE BOTH HANDS

To mince herbs and garlic, grip handle with one hand and rest fingers of other hand lightly on knife tip. This grip facilitates up-and-down rocking motion needed for mincing. To make sure food is evenly minced, pivot knife through pile of food as you work.

"The recipe was really fun to make and a little challenging. I thought the sauce was so good with the tofu, and I liked how the cornstarch turned into a crust in the hot oil!" —Clementine, 12

STIR-FRIED TOFU WITH GREEN BEANS

SERVES 4
PREP TIME: 20 MINUTES
COOK TIME: 45 MINUTES

PREPARE INGREDIENTS

14 ounces extra-firm tofu
1 cup vegetable broth
3 tablespoons soy sauce
1 tablespoon rice vinegar
1 tablespoon packed brown sugar
2 teaspoons plus ⅓ cup cornstarch, measured separately
1 teaspoon toasted sesame oil
2 tablespoons plus 1 tablespoon vegetable oil, measured separately

1 pound green beans, ends trimmed (see photo, page 153)
2 scallions, sliced thin
3 garlic cloves, peeled and minced (see page 13 for how to mince garlic)
½ teaspoon ground ginger

GATHER COOKING EQUIPMENT

Cutting board
Chef's knife
Ruler
Rimmed baking sheet
Paper towels
2 medium bowls
Whisk
Rubber spatula
12-inch nonstick skillet with lid
Large plate
Oven mitts

1. Use chef's knife to cut tofu into ¾-inch cubes (see photos, right). Line rimmed baking sheet with three layers of paper towels. Spread tofu cubes on baking sheet and let drain for 20 minutes.

2. While tofu drains, in medium bowl, whisk together broth, soy sauce, vinegar, sugar, 2 teaspoons cornstarch, and sesame oil.

3. Gently pat tofu dry with more paper towels. Transfer to second medium bowl. Add remaining ⅓ cup cornstarch to bowl. Use rubber spatula to gently stir tofu to coat until there is no dry cornstarch remaining.

4. In 12-inch nonstick skillet, heat 2 table-spoons vegetable oil over medium heat for 1 minute (oil should be hot but not smoking). Carefully add tofu to pan and use rubber spatula to spread it into even layer. Cook, stirring often, until golden brown, 10 to 12 minutes. Turn off heat. Transfer tofu to large plate lined with paper towels.

5. Add remaining 1 tablespoon vegetable oil and green beans to skillet and return to medium heat. Cover and cook until green beans are bright green, about 3 minutes. Use oven mitts to remove lid. Continue to cook, stirring occasionally, until green beans are spotty brown all over, about 3 minutes.

6. Carefully add tofu, scallions, garlic, and ginger to skillet. Whisk broth mixture to recombine, then pour into skillet. Cook, stirring constantly, until sauce is thickened, about 1 minute. Turn off heat. Serve.

CUTTING TOFU INTO CUBES

1. Slice block of tofu lengthwise (the long way) into four ¾-inch-thick slabs.

2. Lay slabs flat and cut each slab in half lengthwise to make 2 long fingers (about ¾ inch thick).

3. Cut tofu fingers crosswise (the short way) into ¾-inch cubes.

RICE AND BEAN BOWLS WITH CORN AND AVOCADO CREMA

SERVES 4 TO 6
PREP TIME: 20 MINUTES
COOK TIME: 45 MINUTES

PREPARE INGREDIENTS

1 ripe avocado
6 tablespoons water
¼ cup cilantro leaves
2 tablespoons lime juice, squeezed from 1 lime
2 tablespoons sour cream
Salt and pepper
2 (15-ounce) cans black beans, opened
1 cup long-grain white rice
1 tablespoon plus 1 tablespoon extra-virgin olive oil, measured separately
1½ cups frozen corn
1 onion, peeled and chopped fine (see page 13 for how to chop onions)
1 teaspoon ground cumin
2 cups vegetable broth
Pico de gallo or salsa

GATHER COOKING EQUIPMENT

Butter knife
Soupspoon
Food processor
Rubber spatula
2 bowls (1 small, 1 medium)
Colander

Fine-mesh strainer
12-inch nonstick skillet with lid
Aluminum foil
Oven mitts
Serving bowls

"I loved making it, and everything was so fun to make! Also, the avocado sauce was delicious."
—Jaden, 9

START COOKING! ←≪≪≪

1. Use butter knife to cut avocado in half lengthwise around pit (see photos, page 37). With your hands, twist both halves in opposite directions to separate. Use soupspoon to remove pit. Scoop avocado from skin into food processor; discard pit and skin.

2. Add water, cilantro, lime juice, sour cream, and ¼ teaspoon salt to food processor and lock lid into place. Process mixture until completely smooth, about 1 minute. Stop food processor. Carefully remove food processor blade (ask an adult for help). Use rubber spatula to transfer avocado crema to small bowl.

3. Set colander in sink. Pour beans into colander and rinse with cold water. Shake colander to drain well. Pour rice into fine-mesh strainer and rinse with cold water until water is no longer cloudy. Shake strainer to drain well. Set aside.

4. In 12-inch nonstick skillet, heat 1 tablespoon oil over medium heat for 1 minute (oil should be hot but not smoking). Add corn to skillet and use rubber spatula to spread it in even layer. Cook, stirring occasionally, until corn is lightly browned, about 5 minutes. Turn off heat. Use spatula to transfer corn to medium bowl. Cover bowl with aluminum foil.

5. Add onion, cumin, ½ teaspoon salt, and remaining 1 tablespoon oil to skillet and return to medium heat. Cook, stirring occasionally, until onion has softened, about 5 minutes.

6. Carefully stir in beans, rice, and broth and bring to simmer. Cover, reduce heat to low, and cook for 10 minutes.

7. Use oven mitts to remove lid. Stir rice mixture and put lid back on skillet. Continue cooking until liquid is absorbed, 5 to 10 minutes.

8. Turn off heat. Divide rice mixture evenly among serving bowls. Top each bowl with corn and pico de gallo. Use soupspoon to drizzle bowls with avocado crema. Serve.

ONE BOWL, MANY FLAVORS

The sustaining combination of rice and beans is popular in many Latin American cuisines. This recipe is a quick weeknight version that uses the rice and beans as a base for a fun bowl with fresh toppings. Cooking the beans and rice together flavors the beans while the rice becomes tender. Topping each serving with sweet corn, fresh salsa, and a tangy avocado sauce completes this exciting one-bowl meal.

SWEET AND TANGY GLAZED SALMON

SERVES 4
PREP TIME: 10 MINUTES
COOK TIME: 25 MINUTES

PREPARE INGREDIENTS

¼ cup maple syrup
2 tablespoons balsamic vinegar
2 tablespoons soy sauce
1 tablespoon lime juice,
    squeezed from 1 lime
2 garlic cloves, peeled and
    minced (see page 13 for how
    to mince garlic)
Salt and pepper
4 (6-ounce) skin-on salmon fillets
1 lime, cut into wedges

GATHER COOKING EQUIPMENT

Medium saucepan
12-inch nonstick skillet
Tongs
Spatula
Instant-read thermometer
Serving platter
Aluminum foil
Rubber spatula
Large spoon

"I thought it was cool because I've never cooked something in a stovetop pan. I learned how to peel and mince garlic. This is very useful." —Greta, 10

"Simple to understand. Also, it was very delicious and even my picky brother liked it." —Cohen, 10

START COOKING!

1. In medium saucepan, combine maple syrup, vinegar, soy sauce, lime juice, and garlic. Set aside.

2. In 12-inch nonstick skillet, sprinkle ¼ teaspoon salt and ¼ teaspoon pepper in even layer. Place salmon fillets, skin side down, in skillet. Wash your hands. Sprinkle tops of fillets with ¼ teaspoon salt and ⅛ teaspoon pepper.

3. Cook salmon over medium heat, without moving salmon, until fat begins to puddle around fillets and skin begins to brown, 6 to 8 minutes.

4. Use tongs and spatula to carefully flip fillets (see photo, right). Cook, without moving fillets, until center of each fillet registers 125 degrees on instant-read thermometer, 6 to 8 minutes. (See page 117 for how to use thermometer.) Turn off heat. Transfer fillets, skin side down, to serving platter. Cover platter with aluminum foil.

5. Cook maple syrup mixture in saucepan over medium heat, stirring occasionally with rubber spatula, until thick and syrupy, 4 to 6 minutes (sauce will be very bubbly when it thickens). Turn off heat. Spoon glaze evenly over salmon. Serve with lime wedges.

HOW TO FLIP FISH

Gently slide spatula under fish to loosen skin from skillet, then use tongs to flip fish.

A COLD START FOR SALMON

Starting salmon with the skin side down in a cold pan is a neat way to cook fish. The skin protects the fish from drying out. The skin also releases fat into the pan, which is then used to cook the second side until it is golden brown, no extra oil needed. To help keep the fish from sticking and allow the fat to puddle under the fish (and not just around it), sprinkle a thin layer of salt and pepper over the cold pan before adding the fish. And make sure to use a nonstick pan.

"Much yummier than I thought it would be. I loved the buttered breadcrumb crunch on top!" —Jack, 9

CRISPY BAKED COD

SERVES 4
PREP TIME: 15 MINUTES
COOK TIME: 50 MINUTES

PREPARE INGREDIENTS

Vegetable oil spray
2 tablespoons unsalted butter
¾ cup panko bread crumbs
2 garlic cloves, peeled and minced
    (see page 13 for how to mince garlic)
Salt and pepper
2 tablespoons minced fresh parsley
    (see page 13 for how to mince herbs)
2 tablespoons mayonnaise
1 large egg yolk (see page 12 for how
    to separate eggs)
½ teaspoon grated lemon zest, plus
    lemon wedges (see page 14 for how
    to grate zest)
4 (6-ounce) skinless cod fillets, 1 to 1½
    inches thick

GATHER COOKING EQUIPMENT

Rimmed baking sheet
Aluminum foil
2 cooling racks
12-inch skillet
Rubber spatula
2 bowls (1 medium, 1 small)
Whisk
Paper towels
Small spoon
Instant-read thermometer
Oven mitts

1. Adjust oven rack to middle position and heat oven to 300 degrees. Line rimmed baking sheet with aluminum foil and set cooling rack inside baking sheet. Spray rack with vegetable oil spray.

2. In 12-inch skillet, melt butter over medium heat. Add panko, garlic, ½ teaspoon salt, and ¼ teaspoon pepper and cook, stirring often with rubber spatula, until lightly browned, 3 to 5 minutes.

3. Turn off heat. Transfer panko mixture to medium bowl. Stir in parsley and let cool for 10 minutes.

4. Meanwhile, in small bowl, whisk together mayonnaise, egg yolk, and lemon zest.

5. Use paper towels to pat fish dry. Use back of small spoon to spread mayonnaise mixture evenly over top of each fillet.

6. Working with 1 fillet at a time, coat top of each fillet with panko mixture (see photo, right). Place fillets, crumb side up, on greased rack in baking sheet. Wash your hands.

7. Place baking sheet in oven and bake until fish registers 145 degrees on instant-read thermometer, 30 to 40 minutes. (See page 117 for how to use thermometer.)

8. Use oven mitts to remove baking sheet from oven (ask an adult for help). Place baking sheet on second cooling rack. Serve fish with lemon wedges.

COATING FISH

Dip mayonnaise-coated side of fish into panko mixture. Press crumbs so they stick to fish. Just coat top side—any crumbs on bottom of fish will get soggy in oven.

LOW AND SLOW IS THE WAY TO GO

A low-temperature oven (set to just 300 degrees) ensures that the fish cooks slowly, without drying out. Crispy, buttery, garlicky panko bread crumbs get a head start in a skillet so they're golden brown when the fish comes out of the oven. Finally, a mayonnaise and egg yolk "glue" adds rich flavor and helps the crumb topping stay put. Even kids who don't usually like fish will like this dish!

BEEF AND BEAN CHILI

SERVES 6
PREP TIME: 20 MINUTES
COOK TIME: 1 HOUR

PREPARE INGREDIENTS

1 pound 85 percent lean ground beef
2 tablespoons water
¼ teaspoon baking soda
1 (15-ounce) can pinto beans, opened
3 tablespoons vegetable oil
1 small onion, peeled and chopped
   (see page 13 for how to chop onions)
1 red bell pepper, stemmed, seeded,
   and cut into ½-inch pieces (see photos,
   right)
¼ teaspoon salt
4 garlic cloves, peeled and minced
   (see page 13 for how to mince garlic)
3 tablespoons chili powder
2 teaspoons ground cumin
¾ teaspoon dried oregano
1½ cups chicken broth
1 (14.5-ounce) can crushed tomatoes,
   opened

GATHER COOKING EQUIPMENT

2 bowls (1 medium,   Wooden spoon
   1 small)   Oven mitts
Rubber spatula   Ladle
Colander   Serving bowls
Dutch oven with lid

"It was amazing. My dad had four servings."
—Zoe, 10

SECRET INGREDIENT: BAKING SODA

Ground beef is an easy base for chili as it doesn't require any preparation such as chopping or slicing beforehand—just put it in the pot and go! This convenience comes at a price, however, as ground meat can give up a lot of moisture as it cooks and becomes dry and pebbly. To keep the beef tender and moist, treat it with baking soda. Yes, baking soda! The baking soda raises the meat's pH, helping its proteins attract more water and lock it in during cooking. This keeps the meat juicy and also helps it brown more quickly.

FAVORITE CHILI TOPPINGS

Serve with your favorite chili toppings, such as **pickled jalapeños**, **shredded cheese**, **sour cream**, **diced avocado** (see page 37 for how to pit an avocado), **chopped cilantro**, or **crushed tortilla chips**.

START COOKING!

1. In medium bowl, combine beef, water, and baking soda. Use rubber spatula to mix until well combined. Set aside.

2. Set colander in sink. Pour beans into colander. Rinse beans with cold water and shake colander to drain well.

3. In Dutch oven, heat oil over medium heat for 1 minute (oil should be hot but not smoking). Add onion, bell pepper, and salt and cook, stirring occasionally with wooden spoon, until vegetables are softened, about 5 minutes. Stir in garlic, chili powder, cumin, and oregano and cook for 1 minute.

4. Add beef mixture and cook, breaking up meat into small pieces with wooden spoon, until no longer pink, about 5 minutes.

5. Carefully stir in broth, tomatoes, and drained beans. Use wooden spoon to scrape up any browned bits on bottom of Dutch oven. Bring to simmer. Reduce heat to medium-low, cover, and cook for 20 minutes, stirring once halfway through (use oven mitts to handle hot lid).

6. Remove lid and continue to cook, stirring occasionally, until chili is thickened, about 20 minutes. Turn off heat. Ladle chili into bowls and serve.

HOW TO CHOP BELL PEPPERS

1. Use chef's knife to slice off top and bottom of pepper. Remove seeds and stem.

2. Slice down through side of pepper. Press pepper so that it lays flat on cutting board.

3. Slice pepper into ½-inch-wide strips. Turn strips and cut crosswise into ½-inch pieces.

SHEET PAN PIZZA

SERVES 4 TO 6
PREP TIME: 15 MINUTES
COOK TIME: 2½ HOURS

PREPARE INGREDIENTS

Vegetable oil spray
2 tablespoons plus 1 tablespoon extra-
    virgin olive oil, measured separately
1 pound pizza dough, room
    temperature (store-bought or see
    page 136 to make your own)
1 (14.5-ounce) can whole peeled
    tomatoes, opened
1 garlic clove, peeled
½ teaspoon red wine vinegar
½ teaspoon dried oregano
¼ teaspoon salt
⅛ teaspoon pepper
2 cups shredded mozzarella cheese
¼ cup grated Parmesan cheese

GATHER COOKING EQUIPMENT

Rimmed baking sheet
Pastry brush
Ruler
Plastic wrap
Colander
Food processor
Medium bowl
Large spoon
Oven mitts
Cooling rack
Spatula
Cutting board
Pizza wheel or chef's knife

"It was delicious! The crust was very crispy, which was my favorite part." —Zoe, 11

"The tomato sauce is really yummy!" —Robert, 11

1. Spray rimmed baking sheet with vegetable oil spray. Use pastry brush to evenly coat baking sheet with 2 tablespoons oil.

2. Place pizza dough on greased baking sheet and turn to coat with oil on both sides. Use your hands to pat and stretch dough into 10-by-6-inch rectangle. Cover with plastic wrap and let rise in warm place until bubbly and doubled in size, 1 to 1½ hours.

3. Use your hands to gently pat and stretch dough into corners of baking sheet (see photo, below). Cover loosely with plastic wrap and let rise in warm place until puffy, about 45 minutes.

4. While dough rises, adjust oven rack to lowest position and heat oven to 450 degrees. Set colander in sink. Pour tomatoes into colander. Shake colander and drain well.

5. Transfer drained tomatoes to food processor. Add remaining 1 tablespoon oil, garlic, vinegar, oregano, salt, and pepper. Lock lid into place. Process mixture until smooth, about 30 seconds. Stop food processor. Carefully remove food processor blade (ask an adult for help). Transfer sauce to medium bowl.

6. When dough is ready, spoon sauce over dough and use back of spoon to spread into even layer, leaving ½-inch border around edges. Evenly sprinkle mozzarella and Parmesan cheeses over top of sauce.

7. Place baking sheet in oven and bake until cheeses are well browned and bubbling, 15 to 20 minutes.

8. Use oven mitts to remove baking sheet from oven (ask an adult for help). Place baking sheet on cooling rack and let pizza cool for 5 minutes.

9. Use spatula to loosen edges of pizza, then carefully slide pizza onto cutting board (baking sheet will be hot). Use pizza wheel or chef's knife to cut pizza into squares and serve.

SHAPING PIZZA DOUGH

After dough has risen for 1 to 1½ hours, use your hands to gently pat and stretch dough out to corners of baking sheet. (If dough snaps back when you press it to corners of baking sheet, cover it with plastic wrap, let it rest for 10 minutes, and try again.)

PIZZA DOUGH

MAKES ABOUT 1 POUND
PREP TIME: 10 MINUTES
COOK TIME: 20 MINUTES, PLUS RISING TIME

PREPARE INGREDIENTS

¾ cup very cold water
1 tablespoon extra-virgin olive oil
1⅔ cups bread flour
1 teaspoon instant or rapid-rise yeast
1 teaspoon sugar
1 teaspoon salt
Vegetable oil spray (if not making Sheet
    Pan Pizza, page 134, right away)

GATHER COOKING EQUIPMENT

Liquid measuring cup
Food processor
Large bowl and plastic wrap (if not making
    Sheet Pan Pizza, page 134, right away)

THE MAGIC OF YEAST

Yeast is a living, single-celled organism. It's actually a microscopic fungus! You buy yeast in small packets at the grocery store. The yeast is "sleeping." Mixing the yeast with a liquid (usually water) wakes up the yeast so it can turn flour into bread dough. So how exactly does that work?

Yeast feeds on the starches in the flour and produces carbon dioxide in the process. Carbon dioxide causes the dough to rise, much like blowing air into chewing gum to make a bubble. All those tiny holes inside a loaf of chewy rustic bread? That's the handiwork of the yeast.

Instant yeast (sometimes labeled rapid-rise yeast) is the most reliable option for home bakers. Keep yeast in the refrigerator and check package dates—old yeast won't work.

START COOKING!

1. In liquid measuring cup, combine water and oil.

2. Add flour, yeast, and sugar to food processor and lock lid into place. Hold down pulse button for 1 second, then release. Repeat until ingredients are combined, about 5 pulses.

3. Turn processor on, then slowly pour water mixture through feed tube until dough comes together and no dry flour remains, about 30 seconds.

4. Stop food processor. Let dough sit for 10 minutes. Add salt to food processor and process until dough forms smooth ball, about 1 minute.

5. Stop food processor. Carefully remove food processor blade (ask an adult for help). Transfer dough to counter and knead by hand to form a smooth, round ball, about 30 seconds.

6. If making Sheet Pan Pizza right away, proceed to page 134. Otherwise, spray large bowl with vegetable oil spray. Place dough in greased bowl and cover with plastic wrap. Let rise in refrigerator for up to 24 hours. When ready to use dough, remove bowl from refrigerator and let dough come to room temperature, 1 to 2 hours. To bring dough to room temperature faster, place cold dough in zipper-lock plastic bag, squeeze out extra air, and seal bag. Place bag in large bowl filled with hot water. Turn and squeeze dough a few times until warmed to room temperature, about 15 minutes.

DOUGH WHEN YOU WANT

Pizza dough recipes have two parts—making the dough and then letting it rise. As the dough rises, the yeast is doing its job and creating air bubbles. These bubbles make the dough grow larger—or rise. You have two options for when and where to let the dough rise.

If making Sheet Pan Pizza, it's easiest to let the dough rise right in the baking sheet. At the end of step 5 of the dough recipe, turn to page 134 and get to work. Dinner awaits.

You also have the option of letting the dough rise in a bowl in the refrigerator—you can make dough on Saturday afternoon for a pizza party on Sunday. If using this dough to make Monkey Bread (page 44) for breakfast, follow the refrigerator instructions. When you wake up the next day, warm up the dough on the counter or in a bowl of hot water as directed in step 6.

CHAPTER 5: SIDES THAT MAKE THE MEAL

SIMPLE BREADS, GRAINS, AND VEGETABLES CAN BE THE UNSUNG HERO AT THE DINNER TABLE. WHAT AN EASY WAY TO HELP IN THE KITCHEN!

CORNY CORNBREAD

SERVES 9
PREP TIME: 15 MINUTES
COOK TIME: 45 MINUTES, PLUS COOLING TIME

PREPARE INGREDIENTS

Vegetable oil spray
1½ cups all-purpose flour
1 cup cornmeal
2 teaspoons baking powder
¼ teaspoon baking soda
¾ teaspoon salt
1 cup buttermilk
¾ cup frozen corn
¼ cup packed light brown sugar
2 large eggs
8 tablespoons unsalted butter, melted
 and cooled (see page 12 for how to
 melt butter)

GATHER COOKING EQUIPMENT

8-inch square baking pan
Medium bowl
Whisk
Blender
Dish towel
Rubber spatula
Oven mitts
Toothpick
Cooling rack
Cutting board
Chef's knife

"It was really yummy! I ate it with soup. I made it all by myself except my mom helped when I asked questions. This is my first time baking something."
—Marilyn, 10

CORNIEST BREAD

Adding whole corn kernels (frozen corn is very convenient) to the usual cornmeal makes this cornbread extra corny. Pureeing the corn in a blender (along with buttermilk and enough light brown sugar to make the bread pleasantly but not overly sweet) makes it easy to incorporate while eliminating tough, chewy kernels. This cornbread is great served with Beef and Bean Chili (page 132), Crispy Oven-Fried Chicken (page 112), or Rice and Bean Bowls with Corn and Avocado Crema (page 126). It is also delicious slathered with any of the flavored butters on page 143.

1. Adjust oven rack to middle position and heat oven to 400 degrees. Spray 8-inch square baking pan with vegetable oil spray.

2. In medium bowl, whisk flour, cornmeal, baking powder, baking soda, and salt until combined.

3. Add buttermilk, corn, and sugar to blender. Place lid on top of blender and hold lid firmly in place with folded dish towel. Process until combined, about 5 seconds.

4. Stop blender. Add eggs to blender, replace lid, and process until well combined (corn lumps will remain), about 5 seconds.

5. Pour buttermilk mixture into bowl with flour mixture. Use rubber spatula to stir until mostly combined (leave some streaks of flour). Add melted butter and stir until just combined and there are no streaks of flour. Pour batter into greased baking pan and smooth surface with spatula.

6. Place baking pan in oven and bake until cornbread is deep golden brown and toothpick inserted in center comes out clean (see photo, page 173), 25 to 30 minutes.

7. Use oven mitts to remove baking pan from oven (ask an adult for help). Place baking pan on cooling rack and let cornbread cool for 10 minutes.

8. Use oven mitts to flip baking pan over onto cooling rack to remove cornbread (see photos, right). Carefully turn cornbread right side up and let cool on rack for 10 minutes. Transfer cornbread to cutting board and cut into squares. Serve warm or at room temperature.

FLIPPING OUT

1. Run butter knife around edge of cornbread to loosen it from pan.

2. Gently flip cornbread out of pan and onto cooling rack.

CORNBREAD TOMORROW

Leftover cornbread makes a great breakfast or snack. Wrap any remaining pieces in plastic and keep them on the counter for up to three days. Reheating leftovers just before serving is best. Wrap what you want to eat in foil and place it in a 350-degree oven for 10 to 15 minutes.

> "Bake until golden brown. It added some crunch."
> —Suriya, 12

> "I like anything that's golden brown." —Tatiana, 12

BUTTERMILK DROP BISCUITS

MAKES 10 TO 12 BISCUITS
PREP TIME: 15 MINUTES
COOK TIME: 30 MINUTES, PLUS COOLING TIME

PREPARE INGREDIENTS

2 cups all-purpose flour
2 teaspoons baking powder
½ teaspoon baking soda
1 teaspoon sugar
¾ teaspoon salt
1 cup buttermilk
8 tablespoons unsalted butter, melted (see page 12 for how to melt butter)
Vegetable oil spray

GATHER COOKING EQUIPMENT

Rimmed baking sheet
Parchment paper
Large bowl
Whisk
Liquid measuring cup
Fork
Rubber spatula
¼-cup dry measuring cup
Butter knife
Oven mitts
Cooling rack

START COOKING! ←≪≪≪

1. Adjust oven rack to middle position and heat oven to 450 degrees. Line rimmed baking sheet with parchment paper.

2. In large bowl, whisk flour, baking powder, baking soda, sugar, and salt until combined. In liquid measuring cup, use fork to stir buttermilk and melted butter until butter forms small clumps.

3. Add buttermilk mixture to bowl with flour mixture. Use rubber spatula to stir until just combined.

4. Spray inside of ¼-cup dry measuring cup with vegetable oil spray. Use greased measuring cup to scoop batter and use butter knife to scrape off extra batter. Drop scoops onto baking sheet to make 10 to 12 biscuits (leave space between biscuits and respray measuring cup as needed).

5. Place baking sheet in oven and bake biscuits until tops are golden brown 12 to 14 minutes. Use oven mitts to remove baking sheet from oven (ask an adult for help). Place baking sheet on cooling rack. Let biscuits cool on baking sheet for 10 minutes. Serve warm.

FLAVORED BUTTERS

Spread these amped-up butters on biscuits or cornbread or put a dollop on hot veggies for a tasty treat.

HONEY BUTTER

Let 6 tablespoons unsalted butter sit in small bowl on counter until soft, 30 minutes to 1 hour. Stir in 1 tablespoon honey and ⅛ teaspoon salt until combined.

SPICY SRIRACHA BUTTER

Let 6 tablespoons unsalted butter sit in small bowl on counter until soft, 30 minutes to 1 hour. Stir in 1 to 1½ teaspoons sriracha until combined.

BASIL-LEMON BUTTER

Let 6 tablespoons unsalted butter sit in small bowl on counter until soft, 30 minutes to 1 hour. Stir in 2 tablespoons minced fresh basil and 1 teaspoon grated lemon zest until combined.

→ MAKE IT YOUR WAY ←

Plain biscuits can be dressed up with any flavorful, relatively dry ingredient, such as herbs, scallions, cheese, dried fruit, or spices.

CHEESY DROP BISCUITS

In step 2, stir ½ cup shredded Monterey Jack cheese or mild cheddar cheese and ¼ cup grated Parmesan cheese into flour mixture.

HERBY DROP BISCUITS

In step 2, stir 1 tablespoon minced fresh thyme or ¾ teaspoon dried thyme into flour mixture.

BROWN SODA BREAD

SERVES 6 TO 8 (MAKES 1 LOAF)
PREP TIME: 15 MINUTES
COOK TIME: 1 HOUR, PLUS COOLING TIME

PREPARE INGREDIENTS

2 cups all-purpose flour, plus extra
   for counter
1½ cups whole-wheat flour
½ cup toasted wheat germ
3 tablespoons sugar
1½ teaspoons salt
1 teaspoon baking powder
1 teaspoon baking soda
1¾ cups buttermilk
2 tablespoons unsalted butter, melted
   (see page 12 for how to melt butter)

GATHER COOKING EQUIPMENT

Rimmed baking sheet
Parchment paper
Large bowl
Whisk
Liquid measuring cup
Fork
Rubber spatula
Ruler
Paring knife
Skewer
Oven mitts
Cooling rack
Spatula
Cutting board

BAKING POWDER AND BAKING SODA

Baking soda and baking powder are white powders used in almost every baking recipe. When activated, they produce carbon dioxide—a tasteless gas that causes batters and doughs to rise. Unless you like flat pancakes and squat biscuits, don't leave out the baking powder and soda!

Baking soda is activated when it's mixed with a moist, acidic ingredient such as buttermilk. Baking powder is activated by any liquid. Many recipes contain both leaveners to ensure maximum rise and good browning (baking soda helps with browning, but baking powder doesn't).

1. Adjust oven rack to lower-middle position and heat oven to 400 degrees. Line rimmed baking sheet with parchment paper.

2. In large bowl, whisk all-purpose flour, whole-wheat flour, wheat germ, sugar, salt, baking powder, and baking soda until combined.

3. In liquid measuring cup, use fork to stir buttermilk and melted butter until butter forms small clumps.

4. Add buttermilk mixture to bowl with flour mixture. Use rubber spatula to stir until dough comes together.

5. Sprinkle clean counter lightly with extra flour. Transfer dough to counter and use your floured hands to knead until smooth ball forms, about 30 seconds (see photos, right). Pat and shape dough into 7-inch circle. Use paring knife to cut cross into top of loaf. Transfer loaf to baking sheet.

6. Place baking sheet in oven and bake until skewer inserted in center of bread comes out clean (see photo, page 173), 45 to 50 minutes.

7. Use oven mitts to remove baking sheet from oven (ask an adult for help) and place on cooling rack. Let bread cool on baking sheet for 5 minutes. Use spatula to transfer bread to cooling rack. Let cool for 1 to 2 hours. Slice (ask an adult for help) and serve.

"Delicious! The crust is really crunchy." —Audrey, 10

X MARKS THE SPOT

Slicing an X in the dough allows the loaf to expand evenly in the oven and gives this Irish bread its traditional shape.

1. Knead dough until smooth ball forms.

2. Pat dough into 7-inch round.

3. With paring knife, cut X in loaf. Each cut should be ¼ inch deep and 5 inches long.

QUINOA WITH HERBS

SERVES 4 TO 6
PREP TIME: 15 MINUTES
COOK TIME: 40 MINUTES

PREPARE INGREDIENTS

2 tablespoons unsalted butter,
    cut into 2 pieces
1 small onion, peeled and chopped
    fine (see page 13 for how to
    chop onions)
½ teaspoon salt
1½ cups prewashed white quinoa
1¾ cups chicken or vegetable broth
3 tablespoons chopped fresh basil,
    parsley, or mint (see page 13 for
    how to chop herbs)

GATHER COOKING EQUIPMENT

Medium saucepan with lid
Wooden spoon
Oven mitts
Fork

"Tastes kind of like mushrooms." —Quentin, 10

"I've had quinoa before and didn't like it, but this
is pretty good. I like the herbs." —Ocean, 10

START COOKING! ◄─≪≪≪

1. In medium saucepan, melt butter over medium heat. Add onion and salt and cook, stirring occasionally with wooden spoon, until softened, about 5 minutes.

2. Add quinoa and cook, stirring often, until quinoa begins to make popping sounds, 2 to 3 minutes.

3. Carefully stir in broth and bring to simmer. Cover, reduce heat to low, and cook for 10 minutes.

4. Use oven mitts to remove lid. Stir quinoa and put lid back in place. Cook until liquid is absorbed, 8 to 10 minutes.

5. Turn off heat. Slide saucepan to cool burner and let sit, covered, for 10 minutes.

6. Use oven mitts to remove lid. Add herbs and gently stir quinoa with fork until fluffy. Serve.

WHY YOU WASH QUINOA

Quinoa is one of the most nutritious and delicious foods on the planet. It's one of the rare plants to contain all the proteins the human body needs. Nutritionists call it a "complete" protein because it contains the nine amino acids essential to human health. While quinoa is cooked like a grain, it's actually a seed native to the Andes Mountains. Quinoa has a natural bitter coating that keeps birds away. Washing the seeds removes the bitter coating and is recommended. You can buy prewashed quinoa (read package labels). If in doubt, rinse the quinoa before using it.

Place quinoa in fine-mesh strainer and rinse under cold, running water until thoroughly moistened. Turn off water. Shake strainer to remove excess liquid.

EASY RICE

Rice is the world's most popular grain, no doubt because it goes with everything. Did you know that white rice is brown rice with the nutritious bran and germ removed? Both recipes serve four to six people.

WHITE RICE PILAF

White rice cooks quickly on the stovetop. Make sure to use a heavy saucepan and to turn the heat down to low once the lid goes on so the rice doesn't scorch.

1. Place 1½ cups long-grain white rice in fine-mesh strainer and rinse under cold running water to remove excess starch. Stir rice occasionally with your fingers until water runs clear, about 1 minute.

2. Melt 1 tablespoon butter (or heat 1 tablespoon olive oil) in large saucepan over medium heat. Add rice and cook, stirring constantly, until grains start to look slightly clear on ends, 1 to 3 minutes.

3. Stir in 2¼ cups water and ½ teaspoon salt and bring to simmer. Reduce heat to low, cover, and cook until water has been absorbed, 16 to 18 minutes.

4. Turn off heat and slide saucepan to cool burner. Use oven mitts to place folded dish towel underneath lid. Let rice sit for 10 minutes. Fluff rice with fork and serve.

BAKED BROWN RICE

Cooking brown rice on the stovetop can be challenging—the rice at the bottom of the saucepan burns before the rice at the top is cooked through. The steady, even heat of the oven eliminates the risk of scorching and lets you do something else while the rice cooks.

1. Heat oven to 375 degrees. Spread 1½ cups brown rice in 8-inch square glass or ceramic baking dish. Add 1 tablespoon butter, cut into 4 pieces, (or 1 tablespoon olive oil) and ½ teaspoon salt (don't stir).

2. Bring water to boil in kettle. Carefully measure 2⅓ cups boiling water into liquid measuring cup. Pour water into baking dish and stir to combine.

3. Cover baking dish tightly with double layer of aluminum foil (baking dish will be hot, so be careful). Place baking dish on middle rack in oven and bake for 1 hour.

4. Carefully remove baking dish from oven and uncover (ask an adult for help). Fluff rice with fork, then cover baking dish with clean dish towel. Let rice sit for 10 minutes. Serve.

"Amazing. Fabulously amazing."
—Ocean, 10

"I had five servings! I want to make it again. The flavors were really good." —Gavin, 8

ROASTED ZUCCHINI "ZOODLES"

SERVES 4
PREP TIME: 15 MINUTES
COOK TIME: 40 MINUTES

PREPARE INGREDIENTS

4 zucchini (8 to 10 ounces each)
1 tablespoon extra-virgin olive oil, plus extra for serving
1 garlic clove, peeled and minced (see page 13 for how to mince garlic)
½ teaspoon salt
¼ teaspoon pepper
¼ cup grated Parmesan cheese
2 tablespoons chopped fresh basil (see page 13 for how to chop herbs)

GATHER COOKING EQUIPMENT

Chef's knife
Cutting board
Spiralizer
Kitchen shears
Ruler
Rimmed baking sheet
Oven mitts
Cooling rack
Tongs
Serving platter

START COOKING! ←〈〈〈〈

1. Adjust oven rack to middle position and heat oven to 375 degrees.

2. Use chef's knife to trim off ends of zucchini. Use spiralizer to cut zucchini into ⅛-inch-thick noodles (see photos, below). On cutting board, pull noodles straight and use kitchen shears to cut them into 12-inch lengths.

3. Transfer noodles to rimmed baking sheet. Drizzle with oil and sprinkle with garlic, salt, and pepper. Toss noodles with your hands to combine and spread them into even layer.

4. Place baking sheet in oven and roast until zucchini is just softened, about 20 minutes.

5. Use oven mitts to remove baking sheet from oven (ask an adult for help) and place on cooling rack. Use tongs to transfer zucchini to serving platter. Sprinkle cheese and basil over zucchini and drizzle with extra oil. Serve.

MAKING ZOODLES

A spiralizer turns carrots, beets, and squash into noodles (or "zoodles" when using zucchini). The steps below work with all these vegetables. For best results, use smaller zucchini, which have thinner skins and fewer seeds. The blade on a spiralizer is very sharp, so make sure to do this with an adult. Place the spiralizer on a flat counter or table and push down on the four corners until the suction cups are secured to the counter or table.

1. Cut off ends of zucchini so it will fit on prongs. Secure zucchini between prongs and blade.

2. Turn crank to spiralize zucchini and produce long noodles.

3. Pull noodles straight on cutting board and use kitchen shears to cut noodles into 12-inch lengths.

GARLICKY SKILLET GREEN BEANS

SERVES 4
PREP TIME: 15 MINUTES
COOK TIME: 15 MINUTES

PREPARE INGREDIENTS

1 teaspoon extra-virgin olive oil
1 pound green beans, trimmed
   (see photo, right)
¼ teaspoon salt
⅛ teaspoon pepper
¼ cup water
1 tablespoon unsalted butter
3 garlic cloves, peeled and
   minced (see page 13 for
   how to mince garlic)

GATHER COOKING EQUIPMENT

12-inch nonstick skillet with lid
Rubber spatula
Oven mitts
Serving platter

"I usually hate green beans,
but these were good." —Quentin, 10

"Has a lot of flavor. Not too crunchy.
Not too mushy." —Suriya, 12

1. In 12-inch nonstick skillet, heat oil over medium heat for 1 minute (oil should be hot but not smoking).

2. Add green beans, salt, and pepper and cook, stirring occasionally with rubber spatula, until spotty brown, 4 to 6 minutes.

3. Carefully add water to skillet. Cover and cook until green beans are bright green, about 2 minutes. Use oven mitt to remove lid (be careful—steam will be hot!).

4. Increase heat to medium-high and cook until water evaporates, about 1 minute.

5. Stir in butter and garlic and cook, stirring often, until green beans are lightly browned, 2 to 4 minutes. Turn off heat. Use spatula to transfer green beans to serving platter. Serve.

TRIMMING GREEN BEANS

Fresh green beans can be cooked in a skillet until perfectly crisp-tender. Adding some water and using a lid ensures that they cook through and don't burn.

To make trimming green beans quick and easy, line up several green beans on cutting board and cut off tough ends. Do same thing on other end of beans.

ROASTED BROCCOLI

SERVES 4
PREP TIME: 10 MINUTES
COOK TIME: 25 MINUTES

PREPARE INGREDIENTS

¼ cup extra-virgin olive oil
¼ teaspoon salt
Pinch pepper
6 cups broccoli florets,
    large florets cut in half
1 lemon, cut into wedges

GATHER COOKING EQUIPMENT

Rimmed baking sheet
Parchment paper
Large bowl
Whisk
Oven mitts
Cooling rack
Spatula
Serving dish

"Lemon makes it so much better." —Neela, 9

ROASTING ROCKS

Roasting might just be the best way to cook vegetables. Roasting is a fancy term for cooking food in a hot oven. The intense heat causes excess moisture to evaporate, leaving a crispy, browned exterior. And all that browning makes food taste better. Roasting is a great way to cook cauliflower, winter squash, carrots, and Brussels sprouts. Cut veggies into bite-sized pieces, toss with olive oil, and then spread out on a rimmed baking sheet. When veggies are lightly browned, they are ready to enjoy.

START COOKING!

1. Adjust oven rack to lowest position and heat oven to 450 degrees. Line rimmed baking sheet with parchment paper.

2. In large bowl, whisk together oil, salt, and pepper. Add broccoli to bowl and use your hands to toss until broccoli is evenly coated with oil mixture.

3. Transfer broccoli to baking sheet. Arrange broccoli in single layer, placing flat sides down when possible.

4. Place baking sheet in oven and roast broccoli until lightly browned, about 10 minutes.

5. Use oven mitts to remove baking sheet from oven (ask an adult for help) and place on cooling rack. Use spatula to transfer broccoli to serving dish. Serve broccoli with lemon wedges.

PARCHMENT PAPER IS YOUR FRIEND

Lining a rimmed baking sheet with special paper that has been treated so it can go in the oven without burning (called parchment paper) is a good idea when baking anything that might stick—everything from cookies to roasted vegetables. The paper also makes cleanup a snap. When the baking sheet is cool, just remove the parchment and throw it in the trash. In a pinch, you can use foil in place of parchment (it's better than nothing), but waxed paper is not designed to go into the oven and is not an option.

MEXICAN STREET CORN

SERVES 6 TO 8
PREP TIME: 20 MINUTES
COOK TIME: 35 MINUTES

PREPARE INGREDIENTS

6 ears corn, husks and silk
  removed (see photos, right)
1 tablespoon extra-virgin olive oil
½ cup mayonnaise
¼ cup crumbled feta cheese
2 tablespoons chopped fresh
  cilantro (see page 13 for how
  to chop herbs)
1 tablespoon lime juice,
  squeezed from 1 lime
1 garlic clove, peeled and
  minced (see page 13 for how
  to mince garlic)
1 teaspoon chili powder
¼ teaspoon salt
1 lime, cut into wedges

GATHER COOKING EQUIPMENT

Rimmed baking sheet
Aluminum foil
3 bowls (1 large microwave-safe bowl,
  1 medium, 1 large)
Large microwave-safe plate
Whisk

Oven mitts
Tongs
Rubber spatula
Cooling rack
Serving platter

START COOKING!

1. Adjust oven rack to middle position and heat oven to 450 degrees. Line rimmed baking sheet with aluminum foil.

2. Snap ears of corn in half. Place in large microwave-safe bowl. Add oil and use your hands to toss and coat evenly with oil. Cover bowl with large microwave-safe plate and cook in microwave for 8 minutes.

3. While corn is in microwave, in medium bowl, whisk mayonnaise, cheese, cilantro, lime juice, garlic, chili powder, and salt until combined.

4. When corn is ready, use oven mitts to remove bowl from microwave (ask an adult for help—bowl will be VERY hot). Carefully remove plate (steam will be hot). Use tongs to transfer corn to second large bowl, leaving any liquid behind.

5. Add half of mayonnaise mixture to bowl with corn and use rubber spatula to stir until corn is well coated.

6. Transfer corn to baking sheet (save large bowl and rubber spatula for step 8). Place baking sheet in oven and roast corn until spotty brown, 10 to 15 minutes.

7. Use oven mitts to remove baking sheet from oven (ask an adult for help). Place on cooling rack and let cool for 5 minutes.

8. Use tongs to carefully transfer corn back to large bowl (baking sheet will be hot). Add remaining mayonnaise mixture and use rubber spatula to stir until corn is well coated. Transfer corn to serving platter. Serve with lime wedges.

REMOVING HUSKS AND SILK

1. Grasp green husks from top of ear of corn with your hands. Pull down to remove husks.

2. After you have removed all husks, pull off stringy "silk" still on corn. Don't worry if you can't remove every piece of silk.

"This recipe is unique because of the combination of flavors." —Mark, 13

SUMMER TOMATO AND PEACH SALAD

SERVES 4 TO 6
PREP TIME: 10 MINUTES
COOK TIME: 25 MINUTES

PREPARE INGREDIENTS

3 ripe tomatoes
Salt and pepper
2 small ripe peaches
3 tablespoons extra-virgin olive oil
1 tablespoon minced shallot
   (see page 13 for how to mince shallots)
1 tablespoon lemon juice, squeezed
   from 1 lemon
¼ cup fresh mint leaves

GATHER COOKING EQUIPMENT

Cutting board
Small serrated knife
Colander
Medium bowl
Whisk
Rubber spatula

PITTING PEACHES

Once peaches are pitted, slice them into wedges and then cut the wedges in half following the same method shown for the tomatoes.

1. Cut small slice off bottom of peach to create flat surface.

2. Slice around pit to remove 4 large pieces. Discard pit.

1. Use small serrated knife to cut each tomato in half (through stem end), then remove and discard core (see photos, right). Cut tomatoes into ½-inch-thick wedges. Cut each wedge in half.

2. In colander, combine tomatoes and ½ teaspoon salt and gently toss to combine. Place colander in sink and let tomatoes drain for 15 minutes.

3. While tomatoes drain, cut each peach away from pit, then discard pit (see photos, left). Slice peaches into ½-inch-thick wedges. Cut each wedge in half.

4. In medium bowl, whisk together oil, shallot, lemon juice, ¼ teaspoon salt, and ⅛ teaspoon pepper. Add drained tomatoes and peaches to bowl with dressing and use rubber spatula to gently stir to combine.

5. With your fingers, tear mint leaves into pieces. Sprinkle mint over salad. Serve.

TASTE OF SUMMER

This recipe is designed for peak-of-the-season, perfectly ripe tomatoes and peaches from your garden or a local farm. It's perfect for heirloom fruits—a term used to describe varieties that can't withstand the rigors of long-distance shipping and are therefore locally grown and readily found at farmers' markets. If you like, serve this salad with crusty bread to sop up the dressing.

TOMATO PREP

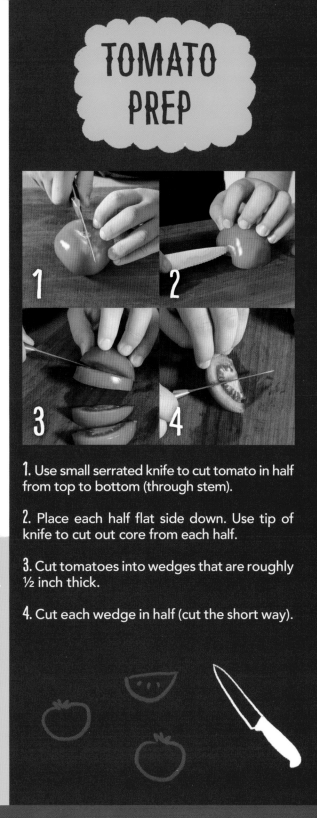

1. Use small serrated knife to cut tomato in half from top to bottom (through stem).

2. Place each half flat side down. Use tip of knife to cut out core from each half.

3. Cut tomatoes into wedges that are roughly ½ inch thick.

4. Cut each wedge in half (cut the short way).

"I thought it was to die for! It was easy. They smelled so good, just like the french fries at Five Guys. We all loved the crispy bottoms and creamy centers. I can't wait to make them again." —Alex, 12

ROASTED FINGERLING POTATOES

SERVES 4 TO 6
PREP TIME: 10 MINUTES
COOK TIME: 50 MINUTES

PREPARE INGREDIENTS

2 pounds fingerling or small red potatoes, cut in half lengthwise (see photo, right)
2 tablespoons extra-virgin olive oil
½ teaspoon salt
¼ teaspoon pepper

GATHER COOKING EQUIPMENT

Rimmed baking sheet
Parchment paper
Large bowl
Oven mitts
Cooling rack
Spatula
Serving platter

SAUCY POTATOES!

Forget the ketchup. Serve roasted potatoes with either of these creamy sauces. They both are great with Baked Sweet Potatoes (page 162), too.

CHIVE SOUR CREAM

In small bowl, stir together ½ cup sour cream, 1 tablespoon minced fresh chives, and ⅛ teaspoon salt. For extra zing, stir in 1 minced garlic clove.

GARAM MASALA YOGURT

In small bowl, stir together ½ cup plain yogurt, 2 teaspoons lemon juice, ½ teaspoon garam masala, and ⅛ teaspoon salt.

START COOKING! ←≪≪≪

1. Adjust oven rack to lowest position and heat oven to 450 degrees. Line rimmed baking sheet with parchment paper.

2. In large bowl, combine potatoes, oil, salt, and pepper. Use your hands to toss potatoes and coat evenly with oil and seasonings.

3. Transfer potatoes to baking sheet. Turn each potato cut side down and spread potatoes into single layer.

4. Place baking sheet in oven and bake until skins are wrinkled and spotty brown, 30 to 35 minutes.

5. Use oven mitts to remove baking sheet from oven (ask an adult for help). Place baking sheet on cooling rack and let cool for 5 minutes. Use spatula to carefully transfer potatoes to serving platter (baking sheet will be hot). Serve.

≡ HALVING POTATOES ≡

Fingerlings are knobby little potatoes that look like your fingers—well, sort of. When roasted, they have a creamy texture and a buttery flavor. If you can't find fingerling potatoes, use small red potatoes instead.

Hold potato steady with your fingers. Use paring knife to slice potato in half lengthwise (the long way).

"Delicious and bursting with flavor. Very simple and easy. I would definitely make this again!" —Jadeyn, 13

"It was fun to make. I enjoyed stabbing the potatoes." —Henry, 9

BAKED SWEET POTATOES

SERVES 4
PREP TIME: 5 MINUTES
COOK TIME: 1 HOUR 25 MINUTES

PREPARE INGREDIENTS

Vegetable oil spray
4 small sweet potatoes (about 8 ounces each)
½ teaspoon salt
¼ teaspoon pepper

GATHER COOKING EQUIPMENT

Rimmed baking sheet
Aluminum foil
2 cooling racks
Fork
Large microwave-safe plate
Tongs
Oven mitts
Dish towel
Paring knife
Serving platter

1. Adjust oven rack to middle position and heat oven to 425 degrees. Line rimmed baking sheet with aluminum foil. Set cooling rack inside baking sheet and spray rack with vegetable oil spray.

2. Use fork to prick each sweet potato lightly in 3 places. Place potatoes on large microwave-safe plate and cook in microwave for 3 minutes.

3. Use tongs to flip potatoes over. Cook in microwave until slightly soft when squeezed with tongs, about 3 minutes.

4. Use oven mitts to remove plate from microwave (ask an adult for help—plate will be VERY hot). Use tongs to transfer potatoes to baking sheet.

5. Place baking sheet in oven and bake until potatoes are lightly browned and feel very soft when gently squeezed with tongs, about 1 hour.

6. Use oven mitts to remove baking sheet from oven (ask an adult for help). Place baking sheet on second cooling rack and let cool for 10 minutes.

7. Use dish towel to hold potato steady and carefully use paring knife to cut slit in potato lengthwise (see photos, right). Use dish towel to hold ends of potato and squeeze slightly to push flesh up and out of slit. Repeat with remaining potatoes. Use tongs to transfer potatoes to serving platter. Sprinkle with salt and pepper. Serve as is or with one of the creamy sauces on page 161.

PRETTY POTATOES

Opening up baked sweet potatoes (or regular potatoes) allows excess steam to escape and gives you a chance to add some sauce, butter, or olive oil. Ask an adult for help—the steam will be hot.

1. Hold sweet potato steady with dish towel. Carefully cut slit in potato.

2. Use dish towel to hold potato and squeeze to push flesh up and out of slit.

SMASHED POTATOES

SERVES 4 TO 6
PREP TIME: 10 MINUTES
COOK TIME: 1 HOUR

PREPARE INGREDIENTS

¼ cup cream cheese
2 pounds small red potatoes, unpeeled
Salt and pepper
1 bay leaf
2 tablespoons unsalted butter, melted
   (see page 12 for how to melt butter)
2 tablespoons chopped fresh chives
   (see page 13 for how to chop herbs)

GATHER COOKING EQUIPMENT

Medium bowl
Large saucepan
Paring knife
Ladle
Liquid measuring cup
Colander
Whisk
Wooden spoon

"Potatoes were tasty. My brothers liked them. The cream cheese made them creamy."
—Anthony, 10

"Recipe was easy to follow. Hardest part was being patient and waiting for the potatoes to cook."
—Finlay, 10

START COOKING! ←‹‹‹‹‹

1. Place cream cheese in medium bowl and let soften on counter.

2. Meanwhile, place potatoes in large saucepan and cover completely with cold water. Add 1 teaspoon salt and bay leaf.

3. Bring to boil over high heat. Reduce heat to medium-low and simmer gently until potatoes are soft and paring knife can be inserted very easily into potatoes, 35 to 45 minutes.

4. Turn off heat. Use ladle to carefully measure ¼ cup cooking water from saucepan into liquid measuring cup and set aside.

5. Carefully drain potatoes in colander set in sink (ask an adult for help). Discard bay leaf. Return potatoes to empty warm saucepan and let sit, uncovered, until potatoes look dry, about 5 minutes.

6. While potatoes dry, add melted butter, chives, reserved cooking water, ½ teaspoon salt, and ⅛ teaspoon pepper to softened cream cheese and whisk until smooth.

7. Use back of wooden spoon to smash potatoes in saucepan just enough to break skins (see photos, right). Don't work potatoes too much (finished dish should be chunky).

8. Stir cream cheese mixture into potatoes until liquid has been absorbed and chunks of potatoes remain. Serve.

SMASHING POTATOES

Smashing red potatoes is so much easier than making traditional mashed potatoes. No peeling or cutting necessary! Potatoes that are 2 inches in diameter are ideal for this recipe. If only larger potatoes are available, increase the cooking time by about 10 minutes.

1. Using back of wooden spoon, smash potatoes just enough to break skins. Don't work potatoes too much.

2. Using wooden spoon, stir cream cheese mixture into potatoes until incorporated.

CHAPTER 6: DESSERTS

CELEBRATE SOMETHING SPECIAL WITH SOMETHING SWEET. BAKE AMAZING CAKES AND COOKIES OR CHILL OUT WITH HOMEMADE ICE CREAM.

BANANA BREAD

SERVES 10
PREP TIME: 15 MINUTES
COOK TIME: 1 HOUR 15 MINUTES,
   PLUS COOLING TIME

PREPARE INGREDIENTS

Vegetable oil spray
2 cups all-purpose flour
¾ teaspoon baking soda
½ teaspoon salt
3 very ripe bananas (skins should be
   speckled black)
¾ cup sugar
2 large eggs
6 tablespoons unsalted butter, melted
   and cooled (see page 12 for how to
   melt butter)
¼ cup plain yogurt
1 teaspoon vanilla extract

GATHER COOKING EQUIPMENT

8½-by-4½-inch metal loaf pan
2 bowls (1 medium, 1 large)
Whisk
Large fork or potato masher
Rubber spatula
Toothpick
Oven mitts
Cooling rack
Cutting board
Chef's knife

"Perfect crustiness at the top, and the sides were a nice mix of crusty and soft." —Ami, 10

"Really fun to make and I enjoyed it! It smelled delicious." —Elle, 10

START COOKING! ←◀◀◀◀

1. Adjust oven rack to middle position and heat oven to 350 degrees. Spray bottom and sides of 8½-by-4½-inch metal loaf pan with vegetable oil spray.

2. In medium bowl, whisk together flour, baking soda, and salt.

3. Peel bananas and place in large bowl. Use large fork or potato masher to mash bananas until broken down but still chunky.

4. Add sugar, eggs, melted butter, yogurt, and vanilla to bowl with bananas and whisk until combined.

5. Add flour mixture and use rubber spatula to gently stir until just combined and no dry flour is visible. Do not overmix—batter should look thick and chunky. Use rubber spatula to scrape batter into greased loaf pan and smooth top.

6. Place loaf pan in oven. Bake until banana bread is golden brown and toothpick inserted in center comes out clean (see photo, page 173), about 55 minutes.

7. Use oven mitts to remove banana bread from oven (ask an adult for help). Place loaf pan on cooling rack and let banana bread cool in pan for 15 minutes.

8. Use oven mitts to carefully turn loaf pan on its side and remove banana bread from pan. Let banana bread cool on cooling rack for at least 1 hour. Transfer to cutting board, slice, and serve.

MAKE IT YOUR WAY

Dress up banana bread with nuts, spices, citrus zest, or chocolate.

→ NUTTY BANANA BREAD ←

Stir ½ cup walnuts, toasted and chopped, into batter along with flour mixture in step 5.

CHOCOLATE CHIP BANANA BREAD

Stir ½ cup mini chocolate chips into batter along with flour mixture in step 5.

TOASTING NUTS

Toasting nuts in the oven makes them taste better. Spread the nuts out on a rimmed baking sheet and heat the nuts in a 350-degree oven until you can smell them, which takes about 5 minutes. Once the nuts cool, chop and stir them into the batter for any cake, cookie, muffin, or quick bread.

APPLESAUCE SNACK CAKE

SERVES 12
PREP TIME: 15 MINUTES
COOK TIME: 55 MINUTES, PLUS COOLING TIME

PREPARE INGREDIENTS

Vegetable oil spray
1½ cups all-purpose flour
1 teaspoon baking soda
½ teaspoon salt
⅔ cup sugar
½ teaspoon ground cinnamon
¼ teaspoon ground nutmeg
1 cup unsweetened applesauce
8 tablespoons unsalted butter, melted
    and cooled (see page 12 for how to
    melt butter)
¼ cup apple cider or apple juice
1 large egg
1 teaspoon vanilla extract

GATHER COOKING EQUIPMENT

Aluminum foil
Ruler
8-inch square metal baking pan
3 bowls (1 medium, 1 large, 1 small)
Whisk
1-tablespoon measuring spoon

Rubber spatula
Toothpick
Oven mitts
Cooling rack
Cutting board
Chef's knife

"I like the spices and it's very fluffy.
It tastes like fall." —Ellie, 11

"Top is really good and crusty." —Ben, 9

1. Adjust oven rack to middle position and heat oven to 325 degrees. Make aluminum foil sling for 8-inch square metal baking pan (see photos, page 172). Spray foil lightly with vegetable oil spray.

2. In medium bowl, whisk together flour, baking soda, and salt.

3. In large bowl, whisk sugar, cinnamon, and nutmeg until well combined. Transfer 2 tablespoons sugar-spice mixture to small bowl and reserve for sprinkling.

4. Add applesauce, melted butter, cider, egg, and vanilla to large bowl with sugar-spice mixture and whisk until well combined.

5. Add flour mixture to applesauce mixture and whisk to combine. Use rubber spatula to scrape batter into greased baking pan and smooth top. Sprinkle reserved sugar-spice mixture evenly over batter.

6. Place baking pan in oven. Bake until toothpick inserted in center comes out clean (see photo, page 173), 35 to 40 minutes.

7. Use oven mitts to remove baking pan from oven (ask an adult for help). Place baking pan on cooling rack and let cake cool in pan for 10 minutes.

8. Use foil to carefully lift cake out of baking pan and place on cooling rack. Let cake cool for at least 30 minutes before serving. Transfer cake to cutting board and discard foil. Cut into pieces and serve.

A SPARKLY TOP

Most of the sugar and spices (cinnamon and nutmeg) go into the cake batter. But in step 3, make sure to measure out 2 tablespoons of the sugar-spice mixture into a small bowl. This gets sprinkled over the batter in the baking pan. In the oven, the sugar will melt into a crispy, sparkly topping for the cake.

Sprinkle reserved sugar-spice mixture evenly over batter right before baking pan goes into oven.

BAKING BASICS

Baking is so much fun, but it does require attention to details. Measuring really matters. In fact, baking recipes are really scientific formulas, so save any improvisation for decorating (see page 182). Learning a few basic techniques will make baking easier.

MAKING A FOIL SLING

Lining a baking pan with two pieces of aluminum foil makes it super easy to get baked brownies, cakes, and even granola bars out of the pan. The pieces of foil should be the same width as the pan and long enough to hang over the sides.

For an 8-inch square pan, both sheets of foil should measure 8 inches across and roughly 13 inches long.

For a 13-by-9-inch pan, one sheet should measure 13 inches wide and the other 9 inches wide. Both sheets should be about 18 inches long.

1. Fold 2 long sheets of aluminum foil to match width of baking pan. Sheets should be same width for square pans but different widths for rectangular pans.

2. Lay sheets of foil in pan so that sheets are perpendicular to each other. Let extra foil hang over edges of pan. Push foil into corners and up sides of pan, smoothing foil so it rests against pan.

GREASING A BAKING PAN

In many recipes, pans need just a quick coat of vegetable oil spray and they are ready to go. Try this trick to keep mess to a minimum.

Hold baking pan over sink. Spray inside of pan, making sure to get even coverage on bottom and sides. Don't worry if some spray misses the mark. It will wash off next time you wash dishes.

IS IT DONE? THE TOOTHPICK TEST

Here's an easy way to test baked goods (muffins, cupcakes, cakes, loaf breads) for doneness. See individual recipes—in some cases the toothpick should come out clean, while in other recipes a few crumbs are OK. If you see wet, sticky batter, keep on baking.

Insert toothpick into center of baked good, then remove it. Examine toothpick for crumbs and evaluate it against directions in specific recipe to determine if baked good is ready to come out of oven.

SOFTENING BUTTER

When taken straight from the refrigerator, butter is quite firm. For some baking recipes and many frostings, you need to soften butter before trying to combine it with other ingredients. This is just a fancy term for letting the temperature of butter rise from 35 degrees (its fridge temperature) to 65 degrees (cool room temperature). This takes about 1 hour. But here are two ways to speed things up.

Counter Method: Cut butter into 1-inch pieces (to create more surface area). Place butter on plate and wait about 30 minutes. Once butter gives to light pressure (try to push your fingertip into butter), it's ready to use.

Microwave Method: Cut butter into 1-inch pieces and place on microwave-safe plate. Heat in microwave at 50 percent power for 10 seconds. Check butter with fingertip test. Heat for another 5 to 10 seconds if necessary.

"Really rich and chocolaty and delicious with ice cream."
—Vivien, 10

"Dense, rich, sweet-but-not-sweet, yummy chocolate cake!"
—Neela, 9

CHOCOLATE SHEET CAKE

SERVES 15
PREP TIME: 15 MINUTES
COOK TIME: 1 HOUR, PLUS COOLING TIME

PREPARE INGREDIENTS

Vegetable oil spray
1½ cups sugar
1¼ cups all-purpose flour
½ teaspoon baking soda
½ teaspoon salt
1⅓ cups bittersweet or
   semisweet chocolate chips
1 cup whole milk
¾ cup Dutch-processed cocoa
   powder
⅔ cup vegetable oil
4 large eggs
1 teaspoon vanilla extract
Milk Chocolate Frosting (page 180)
   or Vanilla Frosting (page 181)

GATHER COOKING EQUIPMENT

13-by-9-inch metal baking pan
Medium bowl
Whisk
Large saucepan
Rubber spatula
Toothpick
Oven mitts
Cooling rack
Icing spatula
Chef's knife

START COOKING! ←—≪≪≪

1. Adjust oven rack to middle position and heat oven to 325 degrees. Spray bottom and sides of 13-by-9-inch metal baking pan with vegetable oil spray.

2. In medium bowl, whisk together sugar, flour, baking soda, and salt.

3. In large saucepan, combine chocolate chips, milk, and cocoa. Place saucepan over low heat and cook, whisking often, until chocolate chips are melted and mixture is smooth, about 5 minutes.

4. Turn off heat. Slide saucepan to cool burner and let mixture cool slightly, about 5 minutes.

5. Add oil, eggs, and vanilla to saucepan with chocolate mixture and whisk until smooth, about 30 seconds.

6. Add flour mixture and whisk until smooth, making sure to scrape corners of saucepan.

7. Use rubber spatula to scrape batter into greased baking pan and smooth top (ask an adult for help because saucepan will be heavy).

8. Place baking pan in oven. Bake until toothpick inserted in center comes out with few crumbs attached (see photo, page 173), 30 to 35 minutes.

9. Use oven mitts to remove baking pan from oven (ask an adult for help). Place baking pan on cooling rack and let cake cool completely in pan, about 2 hours.

10. Use icing spatula to spread frosting evenly over cooled cake (see photo, right). Cut cake into pieces and serve.

FROSTING A SHEET CAKE

A large icing spatula (also called an offset spatula because the blade isn't straight) is the best tool for frosting a sheet cake right in the pan.

Use rubber spatula to mound frosting in center of cake. Then use icing spatula to spread frosting evenly to edges of cake.

WHAT IS DUTCH-PROCESSED COCOA?

A process called Dutching, which was invented in the 19th century by a Dutch chemist and chocolatier named Coenraad Van Houten, raises cocoa powder's pH level, which gives the cocoa a fuller flavor and deeper color. Dutch-processed cocoa (sometimes called "alkalized" or "European-style" cocoa) is the best choice for most baked goods. Using a natural (or "unalkalized") cocoa powder results in a drier cake.

FUDGY CHOCOLATE MUG CAKES

SERVES 2
PREP TIME: 15 MINUTES
COOK TIME: 15 MINUTES

PREPARE INGREDIENTS

¼ cup all-purpose flour
½ teaspoon baking powder
4 tablespoons unsalted butter,
   cut into 4 pieces
3 tablespoons bittersweet or semisweet
   chocolate chips
2 large eggs
¼ cup sugar
2 tablespoons cocoa powder
1 teaspoon vanilla extract
⅛ teaspoon salt

GATHER COOKING EQUIPMENT

2 bowls (1 small, 1 medium microwave-safe)
Whisk
Spoon
2 coffee mugs, (11 ounces each or larger,
   microwave-safe)
Oven mitts

MICROWAVE 101

Most microwaves have a power setting that lets you cook things at reduced power levels. It's important to melt butter and chocolate at 50 percent of full power. The controls can vary from microwave to microwave, but often you have to set the power level before setting the time. Ask an adult for help.

"I'm surprised it cooked through in the microwave! It didn't take long." —Tom, 9

START COOKING!

"Fluffy and creamy." —Celia, 12

1. In small bowl, whisk together flour and baking powder.

2. In medium microwave-safe bowl, combine butter and chocolate chips. Heat in microwave at 50 percent power for 1 minute. Stop microwave and stir mixture with spoon. Heat in microwave at 50 percent power until melted, about 1 minute. Remove bowl from microwave.

3. Add eggs, sugar, cocoa, vanilla, and salt to chocolate mixture and whisk until smooth.

4. Add flour mixture and whisk until smooth. Use spoon to divide batter evenly between 2 coffee mugs.

5. Place mugs on opposite sides of microwave turntable. Cook in micro-wave at 50 percent power for 1 minute. Stop microwave and use spoon to stir batter in each mug, making sure to reach bottom of mug.

6. Cook in microwave at 50 percent power for 1 minute (batter will rise to just below rim of mug and cake should look slightly wet around edges—if top still looks very wet, cook in microwave at 50 percent power for another 15 to 30 seconds).

7. Use oven mitts to remove mugs from microwave and let cool for 5 minutes. Serve warm.

CAKE IN 15 MINUTES

These individual cakes are cooked in coffee mugs in the microwave for a nearly instant dessert—no need for an oven or pan. Microwaving the cakes at 50 percent power is the key to gentle cooking, and stirring halfway through ensures even cooking. If you're using a small microwave with 800 watts or fewer, increase the cooking times in steps 5 and 6 to 90 seconds each. (To find out the wattage of your microwave, check the label inside the cooking chamber.) These fudgy cakes must be served warm. Add whipped cream or a small scoop of ice cream for a deluxe treat.

"This is a great recipe! The cupcakes were really tasty." —Piper, 9

"It was an easy recipe for really good cupcakes." —Emma, 10

BIRTHDAY CUPCAKES

MAKES 12 CUPCAKES
PREP TIME: 15 MINUTES
COOK TIME: 40 MINUTES, PLUS COOLING TIME

PREPARE INGREDIENTS

1¾ cups all-purpose flour
1 cup sugar
1½ teaspoons baking powder
¾ teaspoon salt
12 tablespoons unsalted
   butter, cut into 12 pieces
   and softened (see page 173
   for how to soften butter)
3 large eggs
¾ cup milk
1½ teaspoons vanilla extract
Vanilla Frosting (page 181)
   or Milk Chocolate Frosting
   (page 180)

GATHER COOKING EQUIPMENT

12-cup muffin tin
12 paper cupcake liners
Large bowl
Whisk
Electric mixer
⅓-cup dry measuring cup
Rubber spatula
Toothpick
Oven mitts
Cooling rack
Small icing spatula or spoon

1. Adjust oven rack to middle position and heat oven to 350 degrees. Line 12-cup muffin tin with 12 paper liners.

2. In large bowl, whisk together flour, sugar, baking powder, and salt.

3. Add butter, one piece at a time, and beat with electric mixer on low speed until mixture resembles coarse sand, about 1 minute.

4. Add eggs, one at a time, and beat until combined.

5. Add milk and vanilla, increase speed to medium, and beat until light and fluffy, and no lumps remain, about 2 minutes.

6. Use ⅓-cup dry measuring cup to divide batter evenly among muffin tin cups (use rubber spatula to scrape batter from measuring cup if needed).

7. Place muffin tin in oven. Bake cupcakes until toothpick inserted in center comes out clean (see photo, page 173), about 20 minutes.

8. Use oven mitts to remove muffin tin from oven (ask an adult for help). Place muffin tin on cooling rack and let cupcakes cool in muffin tin for 15 minutes.

9. Remove cupcakes from muffin tin and transfer to cooling rack. Let cupcakes cool completely, about 1 hour. (If you like, make frosting while cupcakes cool.)

10. Use small icing spatula or spoon to spread frosting over cupcakes (see photos, right). Serve.

FROSTING CUPCAKES

An icing spatula, a small spatula with a bend in the blade that helps keep your hands clean, is best here, but a small spoon will work, too.

1. Mound 2 tablespoons frosting in center of cupcake.

2. Use icing spatula to spread frosting to edge of cupcake, leaving slight mound of frosting in center. Keep frosting off paper liners. Once frosted, cupcakes can be decorated with sprinkles or other treats (see decorating tips, page 182).

MILK CHOCOLATE FROSTING

MAKES ABOUT 2 CUPS
PREP TIME: 5 MINUTES
COOK TIME: 10 MINUTES,
    PLUS 1 HOUR CHILLING TIME

PREPARE INGREDIENTS

1⅓ cups milk chocolate chips
⅓ cup heavy cream
8 tablespoons unsalted butter, cut into
    8 pieces and softened (see page 173
    for how to soften butter)

WE LOVE CHOCOLATE

This recipe calls for just three ingredients but they are transformed by the microwave and refrigerator. Don't use salted butter in this recipe. This recipe makes enough to frost 12 cupcakes or one sheet cake.

GATHER COOKING EQUIPMENT

Large microwave-safe bowl   Whisk
Rubber spatula   Electric mixer

START COOKING!

1. In large microwave-safe bowl, combine chocolate and cream. Heat in microwave at 50 percent power for 1 minute. Stop microwave and stir with rubber spatula. Heat in microwave at 50 percent power until melted, 1 to 2 minutes. Remove bowl from microwave.

2. Add softened butter to chocolate mixture and use whisk to stir and break up large butter pieces. Let sit until butter is fully melted, about 5 minutes. Whisk until completely smooth.

3. Refrigerate frosting until cooled and thickened, about 1 hour.

4. Use electric mixer to beat frosting on medium-high speed until frosting is light and fluffy, about 30 seconds.

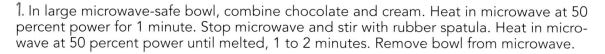

VANILLA FROSTING

MAKES ABOUT 2 CUPS
PREP TIME: 10 MINUTES
COOK TIME: 10 MINUTES

PREPARE INGREDIENTS

16 tablespoons unsalted butter
   (2 sticks), cut into 16 pieces and
   softened (see page 173 for how
   to soften butter)
1½ tablespoons heavy cream
1½ teaspoons vanilla extract
Pinch salt
2 cups confectioners' sugar

EASIEST-EVER FROSTING

This basic frosting can be tinted any shade you want—just add a few drops of food coloring. (A little goes a long way, so use food coloring sparingly.) Don't use salted butter in this recipe. You need a little salt to balance the sugar but not as much as is found in salted butter. This recipe makes enough to frost 12 cupcakes or one sheet cake.

GATHER COOKING EQUIPMENT

Large bowl
Electric mixer

START COOKING!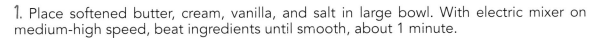

1. Place softened butter, cream, vanilla, and salt in large bowl. With electric mixer on medium-high speed, beat ingredients until smooth, about 1 minute.

2. Reduce speed to medium-low and slowly add confectioners' sugar a little bit at a time. Beat until sugar is fully incorporated and mixture is smooth, about 4 minutes.

3. Increase mixer speed to medium-high and beat until frosting is light and fluffy, about 5 minutes.

LET'S DECORATE

When frosting and decorating cupcakes and cakes, wait until they are completely cool. If they are warm, the butter in the frosting will melt and make a mess. Here are a few simple ideas for decorating cupcakes and a sheet cake. Once you get the hang of it, use your imagination, be creative, and have FUN!

DECORATING CUPCAKES

Once the cupcakes are frosted (see photo, page 179), it's time to get creative.

SPARKLY SPRINKLES

Gently press cookie cutter into frosted cupcake. (Make sure frosting is smooth and choose cookie cutter with simple shape, such as star or heart.) Fill cookie cutter with sprinkles or colored sugar. Carefully remove cookie cutter, leaving behind festive decoration.

FANCY FROSTING

Place frosting in large zipper-lock bag. Using scissors, make small snip, cutting off corner of bag. Hold top of bag (above frosting) with one hand. Starting at outside edge of cupcake and working inward, squeeze bag gently to pipe frosting into spiral, then stop squeezing bag. Pull bag straight away from cupcake to ensure neat spiral.

SHAGGY COAT

Fill small bowl with crushed cookies, sprinkles, shredded coconut, finely chopped nuts, or other topping. Hold bottom of frosted cupcake with one hand and turn cupcake upside down into bowl. Gently rotate cupcake to make sure frosting is evenly coated.

DECORATING A SHEET CAKE

Once the cake is frosted (see photo, page 175), try any one of these tips.

CREATE SWIRLS

Press back of soupspoon into frosting, then twirl it as you lift it away to make artful swoops.

DRESS THE TOP

Sprinkle crushed cookies, shredded coconut, or chocolate shavings over top of cake to cover.

MARK EACH SLICE

Mark each slice of cake with small garnish, such as a berry or nut, or even a piece of candy! When you slice cake, cut between garnishes so that each slice has garnish in center.

PIPE POLKA DOTS

Place frosting (different color than frosting used to cover cake) in small zipper-lock bag. Using scissors, make small snip, cutting off corner of bag. Hold top of bag (above frosting) with one hand. Squeeze bag gently to pipe out small amount of frosting, then stop squeezing bag. Pull bag straight away from cake to make neat dot. Repeat to make more dots.

"I-could-eat-them-forever good."
—Maria, 10

CHEWY CHOCOLATE CHIP COOKIES

MAKES 12 COOKIES
PREP TIME: 15 MINUTES
COOK TIME: 35 MINUTES, PLUS COOLING TIME

PREPARE INGREDIENTS

1 cup plus 2 tablespoons all-purpose flour
¼ teaspoon baking soda
¼ teaspoon salt
½ cup packed light brown sugar
6 tablespoons unsalted butter, melted and cooled (see page 12 for how to melt butter)
¼ cup granulated sugar
1 large egg
1 teaspoon vanilla extract
¾ cup bittersweet or semisweet chocolate chips

GATHER COOKING EQUIPMENT

Rimmed baking sheet
Parchment paper
2 bowls (1 medium, 1 large)
Whisk
Rubber spatula
1-tablespoon measuring spoon
Oven mitts
Cooling rack
Spatula

THE SCIENCE OF CHEWY COOKIES

The classic back-of-the-bag recipe calls for softening butter on the counter, which takes at least 30 minutes. Using melted butter not only is faster but also creates a chewier cookie. Butter is about 20 percent water, and melting it allows this water to mix more easily with the flour to create gluten—the proteins that make cookies chewy. Using a lot of dough for each cookie also makes them especially chewy. Finally, remove the baking sheet from oven when the cookies look almost done. The cookies will finish baking as the hot baking sheet cools.

START COOKING! ←※※※

1. Adjust oven rack to lower-middle position and heat oven to 325 degrees. Line rimmed baking sheet with parchment paper.

2. In medium bowl, whisk together flour, baking soda, and salt.

3. In large bowl, whisk brown sugar, melted butter, and granulated sugar until smooth. Add egg and vanilla and whisk until well combined.

4. Add flour mixture and use rubber spatula to stir until just combined and no streaks of flour are visible. Add chocolate chips and stir until evenly combined. (If dough is really sticky, place bowl in refrigerator for 15 to 30 minutes before proceeding with step 5.)

5. Use your hands to roll dough into 12 balls (about 2 tablespoons each). Place dough balls on baking sheet, leaving space between balls (see photo, right).

6. Place baking sheet in oven. Bake cookies until edges are set and beginning to brown but centers are still soft and puffy, 15 to 20 minutes.

7. Use oven mitts to remove baking sheet from oven (ask an adult for help). Place baking sheet on cooling rack and let cookies cool on baking sheet for 10 minutes.

8. Use spatula to transfer cookies directly to cooling rack and let cool for 5 minutes before serving.

COOKIE BASICS

Use these tricks for cookie perfection.

1. **Line sheet:** Line rimmed baking sheet with parchment paper to prevent sticking.

2. **Stagger rows:** Leave 2 inches between dough balls, arranging them in staggered rows so they don't melt into each other.

3. **Cool on sheet:** Leave cookies on baking sheet for 10 minutes so they can firm up, then transfer cookies to cooling rack.

AFTER-SCHOOL PEANUT BUTTER COOKIES

MAKES 12 COOKIES
PREP TIME: 5 MINUTES
COOK TIME: 25 MINUTES, PLUS COOLING TIME

PREPARE INGREDIENTS

½ cup sugar
1 large egg
½ cup smooth peanut butter
¼ cup M&M's or Reese's Pieces,
   or 12 Hershey's Kisses

GATHER COOKING EQUIPMENT

Rimmed baking sheet
Parchment paper
Large bowl
Whisk
Rubber spatula
1-tablespoon measuring spoon
Small spoon
Oven mitts
Cooling rack
Spatula

"The finished cookie looks like a fancy cartoon cookie. Very shiny!" —Roan, 13

THE WORLD'S EASIEST COOKIE

These four-ingredient cookies are the perfect after-school snack. They rely on the thickness of peanut butter, rather than flour, for their structure. No flour means they are also gluten-free. The candy garnish makes this recipe fun, too. Don't use crunchy peanut butter in this recipe—the cookies won't hold together as well.

START COOKING!

1. Adjust oven rack to middle position and heat oven to 350 degrees. Line rimmed baking sheet with parchment paper.

2. In large bowl, whisk sugar and egg until smooth. Let mixture sit until sugar dissolves, about 5 minutes.

3. Add peanut butter to bowl and use rubber spatula to stir until smooth.

4. Drop 12 scoops of dough onto baking sheet, leaving space between scoops (see photo, below). Gently press candies into tops of cookies.

5. Place baking sheet in oven. Bake cookies until edges are golden and tops are set, 10 to 12 minutes.

6. Use oven mitts to remove baking sheet from oven (ask an adult for help). Place baking sheet on cooling rack and let cookies cool on baking sheet for 10 minutes.

7. Use spatula to transfer cookies directly to cooling rack and let cool for 5 minutes before serving.

SCOOP AND DROP

This cookie dough is very sticky, so use 1-tablespoon measuring spoon to scoop dough, then use small spoon to scrape it onto baking sheet. Repeat process to drop 12 scoops of dough onto baking sheet, leaving about 2 inches of space between each scoop.

BEST BAKE SALE BROWNIES

MAKES 24 BROWNIES
PREP TIME: 15 MINUTES
COOK TIME: 50 MINUTES, PLUS COOLING TIME

PREPARE INGREDIENTS

Vegetable oil spray
1¼ cups all-purpose flour
¾ teaspoon baking powder
½ teaspoon salt
6 ounces unsweetened chocolate
12 tablespoons unsalted butter, cut into 6
    pieces
2¼ cups sugar
4 large eggs
1 tablespoon vanilla extract
½ cup bittersweet or semisweet chocolate
    chips

"The brownies have great flavor and texture.
The recipe was easy to follow." —Anna, 11

GATHER COOKING EQUIPMENT

13-by-9-inch metal baking pan
Aluminum foil
Ruler
2 bowls (1 medium, 1 large
    microwave-safe)
Whisk
Large zipper-lock plastic bag

Rolling pin
Rubber spatula
Toothpick
Oven mitts
Cooling rack
Cutting board
Chef's knife

START COOKING! ←≪≪≪

1. Adjust oven rack to lowest position and heat oven to 350 degrees. Make aluminum foil sling for 13-by-9-inch metal baking pan (see photos, page 172). Spray foil lightly with vegetable oil spray.

2. In medium bowl, whisk together flour, baking powder, and salt.

3. Place unsweetened chocolate in large zipper-lock plastic bag and seal. Use rolling pin to gently pound chocolate into small pieces.

4. In large microwave-safe bowl, combine butter and unsweetened chocolate. Heat in microwave at 50 percent power for 1 minute. Stop microwave and stir mixture with rubber spatula to combine. Heat in microwave at 50 percent power until melted, about 1 minute. Remove bowl from microwave and whisk until smooth.

5. Add sugar, eggs, and vanilla to chocolate mixture and whisk until smooth.

6. Add flour mixture and use rubber spatula to gently stir until just combined. Stir in chocolate chips. Scrape batter into prepared baking pan.

7. Place baking pan in oven. Bake brownies until toothpick inserted in center comes out with few moist crumbs attached (see photo, page 173), 30 to 35 minutes.

8. Use oven mitts to remove baking pan from oven (ask an adult for help). Place baking pan on cooling rack and let brownies cool in pan for 1½ hours.

9. Use foil to lift brownies out of baking pan and transfer to cooling rack. Let cool completely, about 1 hour. Transfer brownies to cutting board and discard foil. Cut brownies into 24 pieces. Serve.

MAKE IT YOUR WAY

The chocolate chips create gooey pockets of melted chocolate in these deluxe brownies. To switch it up, try using ½ cup of your favorite baking chips—such as **peanut butter** or **butterscotch chips**—in place of the chocolate chips in step 6.

CHIP BASICS

Bittersweet chocolate chips have better chocolate flavor than the usual semisweet chips, but either will work in our recipes. Milk chocolate chips are altogether different (they contain milk solids) and should not be used in recipes unless called for by name.

"It has a fudgy texture that's nice like a brownie." —Celia, 12

"It's really, really good." —Elijah, 9

"Smells like sweet butter." —Verveine, 8

BLONDIE BITES

MAKES 12 BLONDIE BITES
PREP TIME: 15 MINUTES
COOK TIME: 30 MINUTES, PLUS COOLING TIME

PREPARE INGREDIENTS

1¼ cups all-purpose flour
¾ teaspoon baking powder
¼ teaspoon salt
1 cup packed light brown sugar
8 tablespoons unsalted butter, melted and cooled (see page 12 for how to melt butter)
2 large eggs
1 tablespoon vanilla extract
½ cup white chocolate chips

GATHER COOKING EQUIPMENT

12-cup muffin tin
12 paper cupcake liners
2 bowls (1 medium, 1 large)
Whisk
Rubber spatula
2 spoons
Oven mitts
Cooling rack

START COOKING!

1. Adjust oven rack to middle position and heat oven to 350 degrees. Line 12-cup muffin tin with 12 paper liners.

2. In medium bowl, whisk together flour, baking powder, and salt.

3. In large bowl, whisk brown sugar and melted butter until smooth. Add eggs and vanilla and whisk until smooth.

4. Add flour mixture and use rubber spatula to gently stir until just combined. Stir in white chocolate chips.

5. Use 2 spoons to divide batter evenly among muffin cups, filling each cup about halfway.

6. Place muffin tin in oven. Bake blondies until golden brown, 14 to 16 minutes.

7. Use oven mitts to remove muffin tin from oven (ask an adult for help). Place muffin tin on cooling rack and let blondies cool in muffin tin for 15 minutes.

8. Remove blondies from muffin tin and transfer to cooling rack. Let blondies cool for at least 10 minutes before serving.

A BAR BECOMES A BITE

Think of blondies as cousins to brownies. They are flavored with brown sugar and studded with creamy white chocolate chips. Like brownies, blondies are typically made in a baking pan and cut into squares when cool. Baking them in a muffin tin dramatically cuts down the baking and cooling time—so you get blondies extra fast!

"Good balance of tart strawberries and sweet cream."
—Owen, 11

"The biscuits are light and fluffy." —Tom, 9

STRAWBERRY SHORTCAKES

MAKES 4 SHORTCAKES
PREP TIME: 20 MINUTES
COOK TIME: 1 HOUR

PREPARE INGREDIENTS

3½ cups strawberries, hulled (see photo, page 199)
3 tablespoons plus 1 tablespoon sugar, measured separately, plus extra for sprinkling
1 cup all-purpose flour
1 teaspoon baking powder
¼ teaspoon baking soda
⅛ teaspoon salt
½ cup buttermilk
4 tablespoons unsalted butter, melted (see page 12 for how to melt butter)
Vegetable oil spray
Whipped Cream (page 197)

GATHER COOKING EQUIPMENT

2 bowls (1 large, 1 medium)
Potato masher
Cutting board
Paring knife
Rubber spatula
Rimmed baking sheet
Parchment paper
Whisk
Liquid measuring cup
Fork
⅓-cup dry measuring cup
Butter knife
Oven mitts
Cooling rack
4 serving plates
Spoon

START COOKING! ←《《《

1. Place half of strawberries in large bowl. Use potato masher to crush strawberries. Slice remaining strawberries and add to bowl with crushed strawberries.

2. Add 3 tablespoons sugar to strawberries and use rubber spatula to stir until combined. Let sit until sugar has dissolved and strawberries are juicy, at least 30 minutes or up to 2 hours.

3. Meanwhile, adjust oven rack to middle position and heat oven to 450 degrees. Line rimmed baking sheet with parchment paper.

4. In medium bowl, whisk together flour, baking powder, baking soda, salt, and remaining 1 tablespoon sugar.

5. In liquid measuring cup, use fork to stir buttermilk and melted butter until butter forms small clumps.

6. Add buttermilk mixture to bowl with flour mixture. Use clean rubber spatula to stir until combined.

7. Spray inside of ⅓-cup dry measuring cup with vegetable oil spray. Use greased measuring cup to scoop batter and use butter knife to scrape off extra batter. Drop scoops onto baking sheet to make 4 biscuits, leaving space between biscuits. Sprinkle each biscuit generously with extra sugar.

8. Place baking sheet in oven. Bake biscuits until tops are golden brown, 12 to 14 minutes.

9. Use oven mitts to remove baking sheet from oven (ask an adult for help). Place baking sheet on cooling rack and let biscuits cool on baking sheet for 10 minutes. (This is a good time to make Whipped Cream, page 197.)

10. Turn biscuits on their sides and use tip of clean fork to carefully split each biscuit in half (see photo, below). Transfer biscuits to individual serving plates. Use spoon to divide strawberries evenly among biscuit bottoms. Top each with spoonful of whipped cream and 1 biscuit top. Serve.

SPLITTING OPEN BISCUITS

You can split open biscuits just like English muffins. Because the biscuits are delicate, using a fork is easier than using a knife.

Turn biscuit on its side, then poke tip of fork gently around edge of biscuit to split open.

"Loved the flavor and creamy texture." —Reece, 11

"Awesome because I really like the white chocolate." —Jonathon, 9

MAGIC VANILLA ICE CREAM

SERVES 8 (MAKES ABOUT 1 QUART)
PREP TIME: 10 MINUTES
COOK TIME: 15 MINUTES,
   PLUS 6 HOURS FREEZING TIME

PREPARE INGREDIENTS

½ cup sweetened condensed milk
3 tablespoons white chocolate chips
¼ cup sour cream
1 tablespoon vanilla extract
Pinch salt
1¼ cups heavy cream, very cold

GATHER COOKING EQUIPMENT

2 bowls (1 large microwave-safe,
   1 large)
Rubber spatula
Electric mixer
Airtight container (1 quart or larger)
Plastic wrap
Ice cream scoop

ICE CREAM WITHOUT CHURNING

Homemade ice cream typically calls for a dedicated ice cream maker for churning. But this recipe uses some unusual ingredients and techniques to achieve similar results with equipment that's already in your kitchen. If you prefer chocolate ice cream, you can adapt this recipe as follows:

MAGIC CHOCOLATE ICE CREAM

Use ¾ cup bittersweet or semisweet chocolate chips in place of white chocolate chips. Reduce vanilla to 1½ teaspoons.

START COOKING!

1. Combine condensed milk and white chocolate chips in large microwave-safe bowl. Heat in microwave at 50 percent power for 30 seconds. Stop microwave and use rubber spatula to stir mixture.

2. Heat in microwave at 50 percent power until chips soften, about 30 seconds. Remove bowl from microwave.

3. Use rubber spatula to stir mixture, smearing chips against side of bowl, until chocolate has melted completely, about 2 minutes.

4. Stir in sour cream, vanilla, and salt until well combined.

5. Pour cold cream into second large bowl. Use electric mixer on medium-low speed to whip cream for 1 minute. Increase speed to high and whip until cream is smooth and thick, about 1 minute. Stop mixer and lift beaters out of cream. If cream clings to beaters and makes soft peaks that stand up on their own, you're done (see photo, page 197). If not, keep beating and checking for 1 to 2 more minutes. Don't overwhip cream.

6. Use rubber spatula to stir one-third of whipped cream into white chocolate mixture until combined, then gently fold in remaining whipped cream until no white streaks are visible (see photos, right).

7. Transfer ice cream base to airtight container and press plastic wrap on surface of ice cream. Freeze ice cream until firm, at least 6 hours or up to 2 weeks. Scoop and serve.

FOLDING

Folding isn't just a chore involving clean laundry—it's also a gentle form of stirring that's used to combine a light and fluffy ingredient, such as whipped cream, with a thick and heavy mixture.

1. Stir one-third of whipped cream into white chocolate mixture until well combined. This lightens chocolate mixture and makes folding process easier.

2. Add remaining whipped cream to white chocolate mixture. Pull rubber spatula toward you, scraping along bottom and up side of bowl. Repeat until ingredients are combined.

AMAZING CHOCOLATE SAUCE

MAKES ¾ CUP SAUCE (ENOUGH FOR
   8 SERVINGS OF ICE CREAM)
PREP TIME: 5 MINUTES
COOK TIME: 5 MINUTES, PLUS COOLING TIME

PREPARE INGREDIENTS

¾ cup bittersweet or semisweet
   chocolate chips
⅓ cup refined coconut oil
1 teaspoon cocoa powder
¼ teaspoon vanilla extract
Pinch salt

GATHER COOKING EQUIPMENT

Medium microwave-safe bowl
Whisk

SCIENCE IS SWEET

Chocolate sauce that instantly hardens when poured over ice cream is a treat with a party-worthy presentation. Coconut oil is the secret ingredient that causes the sauce to go from a liquid to a solid when its temperature changes.

START COOKING! ◄─◄◄◄◄

1. In medium microwave-safe bowl, combine chocolate chips and coconut oil. Heat in microwave at 50 percent power for 1 minute. Stop microwave and whisk mixture to combine.

2. Heat in microwave at 50 percent power until melted, 1 to 2 minutes. Remove bowl from microwave.

3. Add cocoa, vanilla, and salt and whisk until well combined.

4. Let cool completely, about 30 minutes, before using. (Chocolate sauce can be stored at room temperature in airtight container for 2 months. Before using, microwave at 50 percent power, stirring occasionally, until melted and smooth, 1 to 2 minutes.)

BUILDING A SUNDAE BAR

Sundae bars are an easy way for friends and family to create their own special treats. Use a muffin tin to hold all your favorite toppings, including sprinkles, candies, mini chocolate chips, cherries, crushed cookies, nuts, and coconut—you get the idea. Add a bowl of chocolate or caramel sauce and a bowl of whipped cream and you're good to go!

Arrange ice cream toppings in individual cups of muffin tin

WHIPPED CREAM

Heavy or whipping cream is a must. And make sure the cream is cold. Use an electric mixer for fastest results, although you can use a whisk and whip cream by hand—be prepared for a workout! If using a mixer, keep the beaters low in the bowl to minimize splatters. This recipe makes about 1 cup.

In large bowl, combine ½ cup cold heavy cream, 1½ teaspoons sugar, and ½ teaspoon vanilla extract. Use electric mixer on medium-low speed to whip cream for 1 minute. Increase speed to high and whip until cream is smooth and thick, about 1 minute. Stop mixer and lift beaters out of cream. If cream clings to the beaters and makes soft peaks that stand up on their own, you're done. If not, keep beating and check again in 30 seconds. Don't overwhip cream.

STRAWBERRY CREAM PALETAS

MAKES 6 PALETAS
PREP TIME: 15 MINUTES
COOK TIME: 10 MINUTES, PLUS 6 HOURS
    FREEZING TIME

PREPARE INGREDIENTS

3½ cups strawberries, hulled
    (see photo, right)
½ cup heavy cream
¼ cup honey
1 teaspoon lemon juice,
    squeezed from ½ lemon
⅛ teaspoon salt

GATHER COOKING EQUIPMENT

Food processor
Rubber spatula
Large liquid measuring cup
6 ice pop molds, about 3 ounces each
6 ice pop sticks

"Delish! Tons of
flavor and refreshing."
—Victoria, 12

"Easy to make and
delicious! Not too
sweet and really nice
strawberry flavor."
—Zoe, 9

START COOKING! ←≪≪≪

1. Place half of strawberries, cream, honey, lemon juice, and salt in food processor. Lock lid in place and process mixture for 20 seconds. Stop food processor, remove lid, and scrape down sides of bowl with rubber spatula. Lock lid back into place and process until smooth, about 10 seconds.

2. Add remaining strawberries to food processor and lock lid in place. Pulse until strawberries are coarsely chopped, about 5 pulses. Carefully remove processor blade (ask an adult for help).

3. Pour strawberry mixture into large liquid measuring cup, using rubber spatula to help scrape out mixture. Divide strawberry mixture evenly among ice pop molds.

4. Insert 1 stick in center of each mold and seal with cover. Freeze until firm, at least 6 hours or up to 5 days.

5. Hold mold under warm running water for 30 seconds to thaw slightly. Slide paleta out of mold and serve.

EASY ICE POPS

A cousin of ice pops, paletas are Mexican-style frozen treats that start with fresh fruit juice as their base and often have chunks of fresh fruit stirred in. The food processor makes quick work of breaking down the berries. Fresh fruit tastes best, but you can use 1 pound of frozen strawberries, thawed and drained on paper towels, in this recipe.

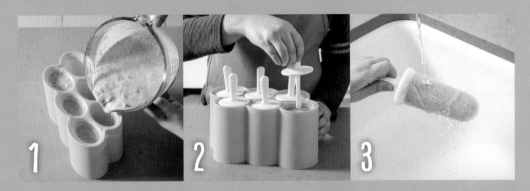

1. Transfer strawberry mixture to liquid measuring cup for easy pouring. Divide mixture evenly among six 3-ounce ice pop molds.

2. Insert 1 stick into center of each mold. Cover molds and freeze until firm, at least 6 hours.

3. When ready to serve, hold mold under warm running water for 30 seconds to thaw slightly. Once paleta thaws slightly, it will slide right out of mold.

HULLING STRAWBERRIES

The hull is the leafy green part of the strawberry. Use a paring knife to remove it as well as some of the whitish berry right underneath the leaves (this part of the berry can be tough).

Place strawberry on its side and use paring knife to carefully cut off top with leafy green part.

CONVERSIONS & EQUIVALENTS

The recipes in this book were developed using standard U.S. measures. The charts below offer equivalents for U.S. and metric measures. All conversions are approximate and have been rounded up or down to the nearest whole number.

VOLUME CONVERSIONS

U.S.	METRIC
1 teaspoon	5 milliliters
2 teaspoons	10 milliliters
1 tablespoon	15 milliliters
2 tablespoons	30 milliliters
¼ cup	59 milliliters
⅓ cup	79 milliliters
½ cup	118 milliliters
¾ cup	177 milliliters
1 cup	237 milliliters
2 cups (1 pint)	473 milliliters
4 cups (1 quart)	0.946 liter
4 quarts (1 gallon)	3.8 liters

WEIGHT CONVERSIONS

OUNCES	GRAMS
½	14
¾	21
1	28
2	57
3	85
4	113
5	142
6	170
8	227
10	283
12	340
16 (1 pound)	454

OVEN TEMPERATURES

FAHRENHEIT	CELSIUS	GAS MARK
225	105	¼
250	120	½
275	135	1
300	150	2
325	165	3
350	180	4
375	190	5
400	200	6
425	220	7
450	230	8
475	245	9

CONVERTING TEMPERATURES FROM AN INSTANT-READ THERMOMETER

We include doneness temperatures in many recipes in this book. We recommend an instant-read thermometer for the job. To convert Fahrenheit degrees to Celsius:

Subtract 32 degrees from the Fahrenheit reading, then divide the result by 1.8.

Example
"Roast chicken until thighs register 175°F degrees"

To Convert
175°F − 32 = 143°
143° ÷ 1.8 = 79.44°C, rounded down to 79°C

HEALTHY EATING 101

Food is fuel for your body and your mind. Food supplies the energy that helps you play, think, draw, walk, and run. Different foods perform different functions in your body, so a varied diet is important.

MyPlate was developed by the U.S. Department of Agriculture to help understand the major food groups. The MyPlate illustration is a place setting for a meal and uses the five food groups to build a healthy meal. For more information about MyPlate, go to www.choosemyplate.gov.

Keep these principles in mind as you build a healthy diet.

- Fill half your plate with vegetables and fruits.
- Eat vegetables and fruits in a variety of colors. Red, orange, and dark-green vegetables are especially good for you.
- Make sure half the grains you eat are whole grain, such as brown rice, oats, or whole-wheat pasta.
- Choose lean proteins and low-fat or skim dairy.
- Drink water or 100 percent fruit juice rather than sugary sodas.
- Eat sweets, likes cakes and cookies, once in a while and in small amounts.
- Be active (walk to school, ride your bike, play sports) at least 1 hour every day.

MAKING GOOD CHOICES EVERY DAY

Use this chart to help plan a healthy diet.

FOOD GROUP	EXAMPLES	EAT THIS MUCH EVERY DAY*	EQUALS 1 CUP OR 1 OUNCE	
Vegetables	Vegetables, 100% vegetable juices	1½ to 2 cups	2 medium carrots 12 baby carrots 1 large ear of corn	1 medium potato 1 large tomato
Fruits	Fresh and dried fruits, 100% fruit juices	1 to 1½ cups	1 small apple 1 large banana 32 seedless grapes	1 large orange 8 large strawberries
Grains	Wheat, rice, oats, corn-meal, and foods made from these ingredients such as bread and crackers	5 to 6 ounces	1 slice of bread 1 cup breakfast cereal ½ cup cooked oatmeal or rice	3 cups popcorn 1 large pancake 1 small tortilla
Protein	Meat, poultry, seafood, beans, eggs, tofu, nuts	4 to 5 ounces	1 egg 2 tablespoons hummus 1 tablespoon peanut or almond butter	1 slice of turkey 7 walnut halves
Dairy	Milk, yogurt, cheese	2 to 2½ cups	2 slices cheese (cheddar, mozzarella, Swiss) 1 regular container yogurt	

*For children ages 4 to 13. Younger children will need less than amounts listed. Older children will need more.

A SENSIBLE APPROACH TO NUTRITION

MyPlate is a great starting point but individual needs vary. Talk with your parents and your pediatrician. Some things to keep in mind:

- **Cooking makes it easy to try new foods.** Kids who cook are more excited about eating well and trying new foods.
- **Eat with others.** Sharing food with others is good for you. Family dinners are especially important. And everyone should help out—from setting the table to washing the dishes.
  Exercise impacts your dietary needs. Kids (and adults) who exercise vigorously every day burn more calories. Athletes need more food to fuel their bodies than people who don't exercise.
- **Age impacts your dietary needs.** Four-year-olds don't need to eat as much as twelve-year-olds.
- **No one diet is right for everyone.** Your DNA plays a role in shaping what food your body needs. Many kids (and grown-ups) have allergies or intolerances that affect the food choices they make.
- **A healthy diet is about good habits.** It's fine to eat cookies or cake on occasion. And it's okay if you don't hit the MyPlate goals every single day. A healthy diet is about what you eat over the entire week or month. It's about good habits—not perfection.

RECIPE STATS

Use the information on the following pages to learn more about individual recipes in this book. Unless otherwise noted, this information applies to a single serving. If there is a range in the serving size in the recipe (for example, "serves 4 to 6"), we used the highest number of servings to calculate these nutritional values.

The information that follows is based on data calculated using the Food Processor SQL by ESHA Research. Using low-fat or low-sodium products (such as skim milk or low-sodium canned tomatoes) in recipes will significantly lower fat and sodium values listed in this chart.

UNDERSTANDING NUTRITION TERMS

Food contains four macronutrients (water, fat, carbohydrates, and protein) and dozens and dozens of micronutrients (vitamins and minerals). Macronutrients make up 98 to 99 percent of the weight of most foods and provide the fuel for the body, so that's where we focus our attention.

Calories: This unit of measurement quantifies the energy-producing value of food. Foods with more calories provide more energy to fuel the body. Two apples have twice as many calories as one apple.

Fat: The body uses fat as fuel and can also store fat for later use. Fat also helps the body absorb vitamins. Foods derived from animals (including meat and dairy) as well as oils and nuts are all sources of fat.

Saturated Fat: This type of fat is solid at room temperature, and its consumption should be limited. Butter, cream, fatty cuts of meat, and poultry skin are all sources of saturated fat.

Sodium: This mineral regulates the balance of water in our bodies. Salt is a main source of sodium in our diets. Consumption of sodium should be limited.

Carbohydrates: Among macronutrients, carbohydrates are the most easily converted into energy. There are several types of carbohydrates, including sugars, starches, and fiber.

Fiber: Some carbohydrates are indigestible food matter that help regulate digestion. Whole grains, vegetables, and fruits are the best sources of fiber.

Total Sugar: This type of simple carbohydrate provides quick energy. Sources of sugar include fruits, vegetables, and dairy. A diet that balances sugar along with complex carbohydrates derived from whole grains is best.

Added Sugar: This refers to sweeteners added to foods, like sugar and honey. This is a subset of total sugar, which also includes sugar naturally found in foods.

Protein: Protein builds muscle and regulates the movement of oxygen and waste throughout the body. Foods derived from animals (meat, poultry, seafood, and dairy) as well as beans, nuts, and soy are the best sources of protein.

	CALORIES	FAT (G)	SATURATED FAT (G)	SODIUM (MG)	CARBOHYDRATES (G)	FIBER (G)	TOTAL SUGAR (G)	ADDED SUGAR (G)	PROTEIN (G)
BREAKFAST									
Anytime Fluffy Blueberry Pancakes	250	10	2.5	630	32	0	10	6	6
French Toast for One	530	22	11	510	65	0	26	14	13
Overnight Waffles	420	17	10	660	51	0	8	3	13
Granola Bars (per bar)	210	13	2.5	55	22	3	10	7	5
Strawberry-Peach Smoothies	220	4	2.5	55	45	4	33	8	6
Cherry-Almond Smoothies	460	22	5	140	58	8	43	8	13
Tropical Fruit Smoothies	260	4	2.5	60	53	4	42	8	6
Mixed Berry Smoothies	240	5	2.5	55	49	6	35	8	6
Kale-Pineapple Smoothies	230	4	2.5	60	45	3	26	8	6
Yogurt and Berry Parfaits	230	3.5	2	90	40	2	27	8	12
Hard-Cooked Eggs (per egg)	70	5	1.5	75	0	0	0	0	6
Fried Eggs (per egg)	90	7	2	140	0	0	0	0	6
Scrambled Eggs (per half recipe)	190	16	7	190	1	0	1	0	11
Avocado Toast with Fried Eggs	460	33	5	450	31	7	4	0	11
Breakfast Tacos with Bacon	200	10	3.5	460	18	1	3	0	10
Cheese Omelet	300	25	13	380	1	0	0	0	16
Blueberry Muffins (per muffin)	280	9	6	170	43	0	20	17	5
Banana-Walnut Muffins (per muffin)	320	12	6	180	47	1	22	18	6
Cherry-Almond Muffins (per muffin)	340	10	6	180	53	0	27	17	7
Chocolate Chip Muffins (per muffin)	360	15	9	170	53	0	29	17	7
Monkey Bread	270	11	5	190	43	0	20	18	4
Overnight Oatmeal with Raisins and Brown Sugar	290	4.5	2	160	57	4	25	10	6
Banana and Brown Sugar Oatmeal	280	4.5	2	160	56	6	18	10	6
Blueberry and Almond Oatmeal	330	12	1.5	170	48	7	13	10	9
Toasted Coconut Oatmeal	360	19	16	160	45	5	11	10	7

	CALORIES	FAT (G)	SATURATED FAT (G)	SODIUM (MG)	CARBOHYDRATES (G)	FIBER (G)	TOTAL SUGAR (G)	ADDED SUGAR (G)	PROTEIN (G)
SNACKS & BEVERAGES									
Real Buttered Popcorn	70	4	2	150	8	2	0	0	1
Parmesan-Herb Popcorn	100	4.5	2	170	16	2	6	3	2
Sriracha-Lime Popcorn	70	4	2	160	8	2	0	0	1
Cinnamon-Malt Popcorn	110	4.5	2	170	16	2	6	3	2
Tomato-Mozzarella Bites	200	17	8	70	1	0	1	0	10
Hummus	120	8	1	330	8	2	0	0	3
Greek Yogurt Dip (per ¼ cup)	60	4	2.5	150	2	0	2	0	5
French Onion Dip (per ¼ cup)	30	1	0.5	110	3	0	2	0	3
Tahini-Lemon Yogurt Dip (per ¼ cup)	60	3.5	1	40	4	0	2	1	4
Tortilla Snack Chips	130	4	1	630	20	0	1	0	3
Pizza Chips	130	4.5	1	490	21	0	1	0	3
Cinnamon-Sugar Chips	150	4	1	340	26	1	6	5	3
Ranch Chips	130	4	1	390	20	0	1	0	3
Quick Tomato Salsa	30	0	0	400	6	2	3	0	1
Guacamole	120	11	1.5	150	7	5	1	0	2
Kale Chips	45	2.5	0	160	5	1	0	0	2
Ranch Kale Chips	50	2.5	0	125	6	1	0	0	2
Sesame-Ginger Kale Chips	50	3	0	170	6	1	0	0	2
Cheese Quesadillas	160	12	4.5	290	10	0	1	0	5
Nachos	260	12	5	590	28	5	3	0	12
Real Lemonade	110	0	0	5	29	0	26	25	0
Strawberry Lemonade	120	0	0	5	32	1	28	25	0
Watermelon Lemonade	120	0	0	5	33	0	31	25	0
Raspberry Lemonade	120	0	0	5	31	1	27	25	0
Limeade	110	0	0	5	31	1	26	25	0
Sweet Iced Tea	20	0	0	5	5	0	4	4	0
Cranberry-Orange Iced Tea	45	0	0	0	11	0	10	4	0
Pomegranate-Lime Iced Tea	45	0	0	10	11	0	10	4	0
Best Hot Chocolate	360	24	14	135	34	0	30	0	8
Peanutty Hot Chocolate	320	21	13	160	28	0	25	0	8
COOKING FOR YOU									
Classic Grilled Cheese Sandwich	560	32	17	660	46	0	6	0	20
Caprese Panini	540	27	10	900	55	1	5	0	21
Veggie Wrap with Hummus	670	33	4.5	550	76	11	10	0	19
Spicy BLT Wrap	560	38	11	1090	43	4	7	1	16
Pesto Flatbread "Pizza"	300	16	5	520	28	1	5	0	11
Ham and Cheese Sliders	420	15	6	1420	49	0	6	0	23

	CALORIES	FAT (G)	SATURATED FAT (G)	SODIUM (MG)	CARBOHYDRATES (G)	FIBER (G)	TOTAL SUGAR (G)	ADDED SUGAR (G)	PROTEIN (G)
Roasted Tomato and Corn Tostadas	230	13	4.5	460	22	1	3	0	6
Crispy Veggie Burgers	380	15	2.5	620	46	4	6	0	14
Baby Spinach Salad with Veggies	150	11	1.5	150	12	4	6	0	3
Creamy Dreamy Tomato Soup	250	15	2	750	26	0	10	2	4
Gingery Carrot Soup	140	9	2	770	14	3	8	0	3
Best-Ever Pasta with Butter and Parmesan Cheese	370	15	7	790	41	0	1	0	19
COOKING FOR FAMILY & FRIENDS									
One-Pot Pasta with Quick Tomato Sauce	440	9	1	960	80	4	12	0	14
Sesame Noodles with Snow Peas and Carrots	400	13	2.5	980	55	2	12	3	16
Pesto Turkey Meatballs with Marinara Sauce	460	25	6	880	26	4	11	0	37
Pulled BBQ Chicken Sandwiches	360	8	1.5	890	38	0	16	4	30
Shredded Chicken Tacos	360	12	1.5	270	34	0	7	0	30
Crispy Oven-Fried Chicken	520	11	3	850	31	0	9	0	70
Turkey Burgers	490	21	7	630	37	0	4	0	38
Apple Cider-Glazed Pork Chops	310	10	2.5	450	11	0	9	6	41
Beef and Broccoli Stir-Fry	300	14	4.5	960	15	3	6	0	29
Stir-Fried Tofu with Green Beans	310	17	2.5	890	27	3	8	3	14
Rice and Bean Bowls with Corn and Avocado Crema	340	11	2	880	53	8	3	0	10
Sweet and Tangy Glazed Salmon	420	23	5	860	16	0	13	12	36
Crispy Baked Cod	300	13	5	450	12	0	0	0	33
Beef and Bean Chili	330	20	6	680	21	6	5	0	21
Sheet Pan Pizza	350	19	7	940	29	1	3	1	15
Pizza Dough	150	2.5	0	390	25	1	1	1	5
SIDES THAT MAKE THE MEAL									
Corny Cornbread	280	12	7	370	37	0	8	6	6
Buttermilk Drop Biscuits (per biscuit)	150	8	5	290	15	0	1	0	3
Cheesy Biscuits (per biscuit)	170	10	6	370	15	0	1	0	5
Herby Biscuits (per biscuit)	150	8	5	290	16	0	1	0	3
Honey Butter (per ½ tablespoon)	60	6	5	290	16	0	1	1	0
Spicy Sriracha Butter (per ½ tablespoon)	50	6	3.5	80	1	0	1	0	0
Basil-Lemon Butter (per ½ tablespoon)	50	6	3.5	0	0	0	0	0	0
Brown Soda Bread	270	4.5	2	700	47	3	8	5	9
Quinoa with Herbs	200	6	2.5	350	29	3	2	0	7
White Rice Pilaf	180	2	1	200	36	0	0	0	4
Baked Brown Rice	170	4	1	200	35	3	0	0	3
Roasted Zucchini "Zoodles"	100	6	1.5	430	6	2	4	0	5
Garlicky Skillet Green Beans	70	4	2	150	9	3	4	0	2
Roasted Broccoli	160	14	2	170	5	2	2	0	3

	CALORIES	FAT (G)	SATURATED FAT (G)	SODIUM (MG)	CARBOHYDRATES (G)	FIBER (G)	TOTAL SUGAR (G)	ADDED SUGAR (G)	PROTEIN (G)
Mexican Street Corn	130	10	1.5	140	9	1	3	0	2
Summer Tomato and Peach Salad	90	7	1	290	7	2	5	0	1
Roasted Fingerling Potatoes	160	4.5	0.5	200	27	4	1	0	3
Chive Sour Cream (per 2 tablespoons)	50	4.5	2.5	80	1	0	1	0	1
Garam Masala Yogurt Sauce (per 2 tablespoons)	20	1	0.5	85	2	0	1	0	1
Baked Sweet Potatoes	170	0	0	410	40	7	12	0	4
Smashed Potatoes	170	7	4.5	300	25	3	2	0	4
DESSERTS									
Banana Bread	250	8	4.5	220	41	1	20	15	4
Nutty Banana Bread	290	12	5	220	42	1	20	15	5
Chocolate Chip Banana Bread	300	11	7	220	48	1	26	15	5
Applesauce Snack Cake	180	8	5	200	25	0	14	11	2
Chocolate Sheet Cake	460	29	13	160	48	1	37	35	6
Fudgy Chocolate Mug Cakes	510	32	18	330	49	1	34	34	9
Birthday Cupcakes (per cupcake)	420	24	15	230	45	0	32	32	4
Milk Chocolate Frosting (per 2 tablespoons)	140	11	7	10	8	0	7	7	1
Vanilla Frosting (per 2 tablespoons)	160	12	7	10	15	0	15	15	0
Chewy Chocolate Chip Cookies (per cookie)	200	9	5	85	28	1	19	19	2
After-School Peanut Butter Cookies (per cookie)	120	7	2	60	13	1	12	8	3
Best Bake Sale Brownies (per brownie)	210	11	7	75	28	0	21	21	3
Blondie Bites (per bite)	220	9	6	100	30	0	21	18	3
Strawberry Shortcakes (per shortcake)	410	23	14	300	47	3	23	14	6
Magic Vanilla Ice Cream	230	18	11	60	14	0	14	0	3
Magic Chocolate Ice Cream	280	21	13	55	22	1	20	9	3
Amazing Chocolate Sauce (per 1½ tablespoons)	160	14	11	20	10	1	9	8	1
Whipped Cream (per 2 tablespoons)	50	5	3.5	0	1	0	1	1	0
Strawberry Cream Paletas (per paleta)	140	7	4.5	55	18	2	15	11	1

INDEX